Citizens Family

WORSHIP BOOK

Prophetic Declarations, Congregational Prayers, Hymns, Spiritual songs, and Just worship songs.

Published by

Wildfire
Publishing House

CITIZENS FAMILY WORSHIP BOOK

Published by

Wildfire
Publishing House

Manufactured in
Milton Keynes UK

CONTENTS

PREFACE

"But everything should be done in a fitting and orderly way."
~ 1 Corinthians 14:40

From our humble beginnings on the 25th of June, 2004 at the Students Union Building of the University of Nigeria, Nsukka, the Citizens Family has continued to grow in our commitment to abiding intimacy with God, His Son Jesus Christ, and the sweet Holy Spirit.

In his letter to the Colossian church, the Apostle Paul admonishes Christians of all ages to sing psalms, hymns, and spiritual songs with gratitude in our hearts to God. This first edition of our Worship Book reflects not only our firm dedication to the use of psalms, hymns, and spiritual songs in Christian worship, but also a firm commitment to orderly worship services.

This book has been many years in the making. Citizens Family, from our very first moments, has always written out our prayers, songs, and prophetic declarations in Sunday worship bulletins. As a result of this discipline through the years, we have amassed a rich collection of hymns, and worship songs from several sources, as well as prayers and prophetic declarations from our own leadership.

The prophetic declarations come from our Shepherd, Rev. Wildfire Divine Favour. Each year, from the founding days of our church, he has faithfully received God's words from the Holy Spirit to guide our thoughts, expectations, prayers, and stewardship. The Citizens Family annual prophetic declarations are said at the end of every prayer meetings by the church.

The various prayers compiled here were written by Pastor Sharon D-Favour, the Shepherd's wife. She has diligently developed and written hundreds of these prayers through the years to serve as our congregational opening prayers. These very inspiring prayers have helped us focus our thoughts as we gather as a family for worship.

The worship songs, gathered from several sources, have been diligently documented for use in our services through the years by our various Pastors, and Worship Leaders. The final form presented in this volume is mostly due to several years of painstaking effort by Pastor Sharon D-Favour to preserve our cherished worship songs. She was assisted in this by others, particularly Uche Blessing Okafor who spent untold hours preparing them for their current book format.

The hymns and sacred songs used here have come from more sources than we can enumerate. Under the ever diligent supervision of our Shepherd, they were gathered and compiled by Uche Blessing Okafor who has been mostly responsible for the crafting of our Sunday Service Bulletins in recent times. Upon her rested the arduous task of compiling all the prophetic declarations, prayers, hymns, and worship songs presented in this first edition of the Citizens Family Worship book.

It is important to mention that we have not always adhered strictly to the original texts of borrowed hymns and worship songs. We have made changes here and there to fit with our faith and convictions. This is in no way intended to berate the work of the original authors. Our aim is rather to present their inspired works in a form that is more agreeable to our current understanding of the realities brought about by the redemptive work of our Lord Jesus Christ.

Now, as we meditate, worship, and pray, guided by the inspirations of this book, may our minds be renewed, and our hearts strengthened by the transforming presence of God and His Spirit, through the name of His Holy Son Jesus Christ.

Amen.

ACKNOWLEDGEMENTS

We thank the composers, copyright owners, performers, arrangers, and producers whose songs have been used in the Just Worship section of this present edition of the Citizens Family Worship Book. They are, so far as we have been able to determine:

Citizens Family Nigeria, Dominion City Nigeria, Christ Embassy Nigeria, Pastor Ucy Gabriel, Osinach Kalu, Frank Edward, Michael Smith, Don Moen, Ron Kenoly, Alvin Slaughter, Darlene Zschech, Terry McAlmon, Clarence McLendon, Israel Houghton, Intergrity Music, Hosanna music, Donnie McKlurkin, Cece Winans, Women of Faith, Vineyard Music, Soundberg, Vicky Yohe, Brian Doerksen, Bob Fitts, Mark Barnett, Pastor Bruce Parham, Bishop T.D Jakes & Potter's house mass choir, Benny Hinn Ministries, Kirk Whallum, Lincoln Brewster, Kirk Franklin, Reuben Studdard, Jennifer Ramsey, Joseph Garlington.

Apologies are offered to any authors where names have not been included in the above list through unintentional omissions or inability to trace; mistakes will be rectified as soon as possible.

1 January 2012

PROPHETIC DECLARATIONS

Towards the end of every year, the Shepherd of the Citizens Family spends time in the presence of the Lord to receive His words for the following year.

A key word he gets from the Lord is the Prophetic Statement for the New Year. This is the prophetic essence of all the visions and promises of the Lord for the New Year. It goes to the heart of what every member of the Family would expect from the Lord in the course of that year.

In this edition, we have included the Prophetic Statements from 2006 till date - 2012.

These are God's promises; thus, they are timeless; their potency will never fade. Therefore, they are powerful to deliver their promises to the believer at anytime.

Declare these prophecies over your life, your business, your family, and your congregation each day.

The current Prophetic Statement for each year is declared at the end of every prayer session by members of the Citizens Family.

PROPHETIC DECLARATIONS 2006 - 2012

2006

God has increased us ten times, God has increased us ten times faster, God has increased us ten times higher here in Enugu.

While this prophecy was city-specific when it was given to us - a year before Citizens Family started in the City of Enugu - it's promise and power can be applied to wherever city or field of endeavour you may be in.

2007

This year by the force of divinity working in me, I shall advance in every area of my life with supernatural speed and influence thousands for God in Jesus name. Amen.

2008

Because the Lord has blessed me, this year I will plant my crops and reap a hundred fold, I will wax great and go forward until I become very great to the glory of God, in Jesus name. Amen.

2009

The Divine power of God has given me everything I need for life and godliness. Through the great and precious promises of God, I shall participate in the Divine nature, and manifest God's glory on the earth, everyday of this year. In Jesus' name. Amen

2010

My heart is established in the eternal Word of God. I have overcome by the blood of Jesus Christ and words of my testimony. I will rise and soar triumphantly above all storms of life and enjoy supernatural testimonies everyday of this year, in Jesus' name. Amen.

2011

I humbly accept the Word of Christ that is planted and is dwelling richly in me. I am devoted to prayer and the ministry of the Word of Christ. This year, planted and rooted in the house of God. My profiting and flourishing shall appear to all in Jesus' name. Amen.

2012

"This year, I will not be lazy; but daily, through courageous and persistent work, I will show my faith to Jesus Christ. I will seek only that which pleases Him, and through the power of His love, I will bring glory to my heavenly Father." Amen.

DECLARATIONS AND RESPONSES

(Greetings to be used at anytime.)

Minister: Discover Yourself!
Congregation: In God's presence

(Before Bible readings)

Minister: Prayer before reading the Bible
Congregation: "Open thou my eyes oh Lord, that I might behold wondrous things out of Thy Word"

(After Bible readings)

Minister: This is the Word of the Lord
Congregation: May it dwell richly in our hearts

Get this Classic Spiritual Resource from Rev. Wildfire D-Favour

19 KEYS TO UNCOMMON SOLUTIONS

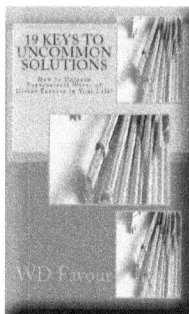

A verse of ancient prophecy declares that the people who survive the sword will find favour in the desert. Favour in the desert refers to the uncommon solutions of the Almighty God. It refers to His supernatural provisions even in the worst of times and circumstances. It is a beautiful description of the limitless possibilities of God.

During an extensive and intensive spiritual journey, which included fifty four days of fasting, praying, prophetic utterances, midnight vigils, spiritual warfare, and so on, God gave Wildfire D-Favour access to the mystery of 'uncommon solutions.'

In this inspirational book, Rev. Wildfire D-Favour shares insights that will help you discover mysterious and supernatural highways through the Red Seas of your life. This is definitely a must-read!

Available at all Citizens Family Church Offices

CONGREGATIONAL PRAYERS

These prayers have been carefully developed from the teachings and messages of the Holy Spirit given to us over the years. They are based on the word of God which abides forever.

Pastors, Home Church Leaders, and other workers within the Citizens Family should use these prayers to guide the thoughts and confessions of the congregation towards God at any point during our worship and other services.

These prayers are also good for personal and family devotions. Use them at any time to direct your heart and mind towards God.

PRAYERS OF ADORATION

CP. No. 1

Holy are You oh Lord! All creations call You Lord. The earth belongs to You; everything in it is Yours. The heavens declare Your glory. The skies proclaim the works of Your hands. Great is Your mercy towards us. You have been our fortress and refuge in times of trouble. You have preserved our lives. Thank You for crowning this year with Your goodness; In Jesus' name we pray. Amen.

CP. No. 2

Immortal and Invisible God! The Lord that reigns supreme in the affairs of men. The foundations of the earth are Yours. You ride upon the ancient heavens. All power belong to You. As we commune with You today, teach us Your ways and lead us in a straight path. Enable us to become one with You in Spirit and truth. This is our prayer, In Jesus' name. Amen.

CP. No. 3

Oh Lord our heavenly Father! We lift up our eyes to You today. You are the father of all creation. Through You all families of the earth are blessed. You water the mountains and the earth is satisfied by the fruit of your work. You are great and most worthy of praise.

Draw us close to You and cause us to abide in Your presence all the days of our lives, in Jesus' name we pray. Amen.

CP. No. 4

Our Father and our God. The God who provides manna in the wilderness and causes water to flow from the rocks. You have been faithful and true in good times and in bad times. You provide for those who hunger and thirst. As we worship You today, may we be abundantly showered by Your blessings, that we may indeed become witnesses for You here on earth. This we pray in Jesus' name. Amen.

CP. No. 5

Everlasting King of glory! The God whose voice thunders over the whole earth! Your voice is powerful and majestic. It breaks the cedars of Lebanon. We enthrone You as Lord in our midst. As we fellowship with You today, sensitize us to hear your voice and may the sound of your voice dismantle every opposition in our lives. Teach us your ways and lead us in a straight path, in Jesus name we pray. Amen.

CP. No. 6

Hallowed be Your name, oh Lord our God! You are the fountain of life. In You our essence is derived. We bless Your name for transforming our lives and giving us new names. You have made us crowns of splendor and royal diadems in your hands. As we call

upon You today, establish the work of our hands, that we may be like trees planted by the streams of water, ever bringing forth abiding fruits in Jesus' name.
Amen.

CP. No. 7

Our help is in Your name, oh Lord our God. You are our confidence and security. You are the Maker of everything. This is the day that You have made. Overwhelming gladness shall be our portion. May the entrance of Your Word cause us to be like a well watered garden and spring, whose waters never fail. May our worship ascend to You as a sweet smelling savour; may the lifting of our hands be like the evening sacrifice. In Jesus' name we pray.
Amen .

CP. No. 8

We lift up our voice to You oh Lord! Who can be compared to You? The God who sits enthroned above circles of the earth; the God who stretches out the heavens like a canopy, the God who measures the waters in the hollow of His hand; the God who created the stars and calls each by name; the God whose wisdom is unsearchable; the God whose beauty is indescribable; the God whose love is unfathomable; the God whose name is majestic. We stand in awe of You, oh Lord! In Jesus' name we pray.
Amen.

CP. No. 9

Gracious Father! The Author of life! Good morning Lord! We will praise You this day with all of our hearts. Our inmost being will give You glory. Your kingdom rules over all. All power belongs to You. Thank You Lord for being our God and restoring our fortunes once again. As we fellowship with You today, may Your metamorphic presence be made manifest to heal, to bless, to prosper and to transform us, in Jesus' name.
Amen.

CP. No. 10

Eternal rock of ages; the Ancient of days; the Lion of the tribe of Judah; the Alpha and Omega, the Beginning and the End; the Author and Perfecter of our faith; the Resurrection and the Life. You are the King of kings, You are the Lord of lords, You are the God of all gods. There is no God like You! You are most worthy of our praise! We give You thanks oh God of heaven, for You alone are great. Be glorified in our midst today, in Jesus' name.
Amen.

CP. No. 11

Blessed be Your name Oh Lord our God; there is no God like You in heaven nor on earth. You are strong and mighty. From the rising of the sun to the place where it sets, Your name is to be praised. As we commune with You this day, captivate our hearts oh Lord! May Your kingdom come in our lives. Establish Your throne in our hearts. Reign in us oh Sovereign Lord! In Jesus' name.
Amen.

CP. No. 12

Heavenly Father, gracious God! You are mighty, Your arm is endued with power. You are our glory and our strength. Righteousness and justice are the foundation of Your throne. As we commune with You today, cause us to receive the wisdom to breakthrough and enable us to stand on higher heights. May we continue to move from glory to glory in Jesus' name.
Amen.

CP. No. 13

Our Lord and our God! Everlasting King of glory! How majestic is Your name in all the earth! You are the beginning and the end; You are the resurrection and the life; You are our risen Lord. We are here to worship Your majesty. As we commune with You today, may every deadness in our lives be quickened by the force of Your Spirit. May every of our unseen realities be unfolded In Jesus' name.
Amen.

CP. No. 14

Glory be to Your name oh God that answers prayers. Your majesty is over all the earth. You are a Father to the Fatherless and a defender of the weak. Thank You for bearing our burdens daily. You load our lives daily with your benefits. As we commune with You today, we confess that our needs will be satisfied in a sun-scorched land and our joy will be full. This we pray in the mighty name of Jesus.
Amen.

CP. No. 15

Heavenly Father, Gracious Lord. Our lips will sing of Your praise today. We are gathered here under the shelter of Your wings and nurtured by Your love. You are the one through whom our lives become holy. Your fragrance overflows and soothes and heals our hearts – consecrating our lives to Your limitless possibilities. May everything else become shadow in the light of who You are. In Jesus' name we pray.
Amen.

CP. No. 16

Jehovah Elshaddai! You are the God of limitless possibilities! You settle the barren woman in her home as a happy mother of children. You raise the poor from the dust and sit them with princes. You turn the hard rock into springs of water and cause the seas to divide at your command. You are the God of Uncommon Solutions! As we worship You today, open our ears and connect us to your frequency; in Jesus' name.
Amen.

CP. No. 17

Heavenly father! What a mighty God You are! There is no mountain too high that You cannot move. No valley is too deep for You to fill. There is no night too dark that Your light cannot pierce. Nothing is impossible with You! As we commune with You today, cause us to be strengthened by the power of Your Spirit, so that we may be connected to the frequency of Your limitless possibilities where every hopelessness

can be turned into beautiful & glorious realities. In Jesus' name.
Amen.

us from simplicity to understanding. In Jesus name
Amen.

CP. No. 18

Blessed are You oh Lord our God; the Eternal King of glory; the Immortal and invisible God; the Unchangeable changer of our times; the God who sits on the circles of the earth. Heaven is Your throne; the earth is Your footstool. We bow in humble adoration before Your throne! You reign supreme in the affairs of men. Be magnified in our midst today. In Jesus name we pray.
Amen.

CP. No. 19

How great You are oh Lord our God! You are a mighty God. You reign supreme over all creation. By Your wisdom You laid the foundations of the earth. By Your mere rebuke You dried up the sea. By Your command You calmed the raging storm. What an Awesome God You are! We stand in awe of You! Thank You for setting our spirits free to worship You; In Jesus' name we pray.
Amen.

CP. No. 20

Blessed are You oh Lord our God. Honor and splendor belong to You. Wealth and glory come from you. The host of heaven bow in reverence before Your throne. We are here today to worship at Your feet, as we fellowship with You today, may the entrance of Your Word into our hearts transform

CP. No. 21

Oh God of all creation. Hallowed be your name. We are honored to sing your praise today. The heavens declare Your glory. The skies proclaim the works of Your hands. Your glory is upon the earth like the waters cover the seas. We are here today to worship your majesty. We have come to declare your matchless worth. You alone are worthy of our worship. What an awesome God You are! In Jesus' name.
Amen.

CP. No. 22

We will praise You oh Lord with all of our hearts. We will glorify Your name forever. You have preserved our lives and kept our feet from slipping. You have delivered us from the depths of the grave. You arm us with strength and You make our ways perfect. We will sing of your great love forever and with our mouths make your faithfulness known throughout all generation, in Jesus' name we pray.
Amen.

CP. No. 23

We lift up our eyes to You oh Lord our God. You are the bedrock of our success. Our inmost being will give You praise. Great is Your love towards us. Your Word is eternal. It stands firm in the heavens. Your kingdom rules over all! Cause us to abound in

Your love and in the understanding of Your Word. Establish Your Word in our hearts today, as we worship You. In Jesus' name.
Amen.

CP. No. 24

Great are You Almighty God...the Lord who reigns in majesty! Your wisdom is unsearchable. You are perfect in power and in love. You are glorious in holiness and awesome in praise. We will praise Your name in all the earth. Breathe upon us afresh and cause our hearts to be strengthened in You, as we fellowship with You and with one another.
Amen.

CP. No. 25

Who is there like You oh Lord? Who can compare to Your glory? Who can fathom the depths of your love for us? You created us in Your likeness. You created us to be Your very own. We stand in awe of You! May Your purposes for our lives be revealed and fulfilled as we encounter You today. In Jesus name.
Amen.

CP. No. 26

Glory to You oh God, now and forever more! We bless You for the marvelous gift of Your life. Thank you for giving us everything we need for life and godliness. Our lives are expressions of Your endless possibilities. Thank You for prospering us and causing us to experience the manifestation of Your

infinite blessings. Give us the understanding to know that we are blessed to be blessings. To You be all the glory, in Jesus' name.
Amen.

CP. No. 27

Eternal Rock of ages! The unchangeable changer of our fortune! The God that has no end and no beginning. You are the same yesterday, You are the same today. You will be the same forever more. There is no God like You, neither in heaven nor on earth. Dominion and awe belong to You. Thank You for the dawning of a new day. Cause us to see the light in Your light today. In Jesus' name we pray.
Amen.

CP. No. 28

Gracious Lord! Eternal rock of ages! The Lord who reigns supreme in the affairs of men! Father of all creation! We are here once again to adore You and glorify Your name. You are our peace. You are our righteousness. You are the stronghold of our lives. As we commune with You today, may we receive empowerment to live and work for You. In Jesus' name.
Amen.

CP. No. 29

Great are You oh Lord and most worthy of our praise! You have made the heavens, the earth, the sea and the springs of water. Splendour and majesty are before You. Satisfy us with Your unfailing love that we may sing for joy and be glad all the days of our lives. May the entrance of Your Word create new realities in our lives today, through Christ our Lord. Amen.

CP. No. 30

Let Your name be praised oh Lord, now and forevermore. You are exalted over all the nations. You are God in all the earth. You make grass grow for the cattle and plants for man to cultivate, bringing forth food from the earth. Your trees are well watered! As we worship You today, make us indeed, refreshing fountains where thirsty souls may drink in Jesus name. Amen.

CP. No. 31

Be glorified oh Lord our God! Our inmost being will give You praise. You are our song. You are our light and our salvation. You are our Shield and the Horn of our salvation. You are our Deliverer. You are the stronghold of our lives. We will praise You among all the nations. Your kingdom rules over all. Receive our worship today, from the depths of our hearts. In Jesus name we pray. Amen.

CP. No. 32

Oh Lord our God. By Your great mercy we come into Your presence today. By the blood of Jesus Christ we have confidence to come to you. We bow before You in adoration. Righteousness and justice are the foundation of Your throne. The heavens declare Your righteousness and all the people see

Your glory. May our tongue speak of Your righteousness and Your praises today. In Jesus name we pray. Amen.

CP. No. 33

We worship You oh Lord our God; You who made the heavens, the earth, the sea and springs of water. You are the maker of everything! To You belong the lifting of our hands. You are our portion, You are our lot, You are our inheritance. You have made our lot secure. As we fellowship with You today, may our hearts be filled with desires for you and may your will be done in our lives. In Jesus name. Amen.

CP. No. 34

Our Father and our God! How majestic is Your name in all the earth! You alone are worthy of our praise! Your steadfast love extends to the heavens! Your faithfulness reaches to the clouds! Your righteousness is like majestic mountains! Your wisdom is like the depth of the great seas! You beauty is indescribable! Saturate our hearts afresh with Your Spirit today. In Jesus name we pray. Amen.

CP. No. 35

Our hearts rejoice in You oh Lord! In You our strength is lifted high. The heavens declare Your glory. The skies proclaim the work of Your hands. We have come to worship You. Your Spirit is like water to our souls. Your Word is a lamp unto our feet. It is sweeter than honey. It is more precious than gold. As we fellowship with You today, bless us with an unflinching desire for You. Through Jesus Christ our LORD. Amen.

CP. No. 36

O most Sovereign God! It is good to praise You and make music to Your name. It is good to gaze upon your majesty. It is good to proclaim Your love in the morning and Your faithfulness at night. May our worship ascend to You as a sweet incense, May it be like the evening sacrifice. We love You Lord. Help us to love You more. Amen.

CP. No. 37

Praise be to You oh God, now and forever more. You reign supreme over all the earth. Wisdom and power are Yours. You change times and seasons. Our times are in Your hands. As we encounter You today, enable us to surrender our lives to you and may our realities be altered to the glory of Your name. We receive grace to rule and reign with Christ once again. Amen.

CP. No. 38

King of glory, King of peace! We exalt you oh Lord our God. You are exalted far above the whole earth. You are awesome in your sanctuary. You are our light. You are our life. You are our dwelling place. It is in You that we live and move and have our being. Thank You for reconciling us unto Yourself and making us partakers of Your divine

nature, through Jesus Christ our Lord. Amen.

CP. No. 39

Oh Lord our God! The One to whom all praise is due. Thank You for being ever present in times of need. Thank You Lord for giving us all that we need for both life and godliness. Today, we cast our cares on You and lay our burdens at Your feet. As we encounter You today, cause the fragrance and the knowledge of Christ to be spread everywhere through us, in Jesus' name! Amen .

CP. No. 40

Oh Lord our God. We have gathered here once again to worship You. Our fellowship is with You and our Lord Jesus Christ. As we lift our hands to You, it is an offering to You. You have liberated our spirits to praise and worship you. Thank You for bringing into us Your banquet hall. Our lives will be filled with Your bounties this day and forever more, through Jesus Christ our Lord. Amen.

CP. No. 41

Heavenly Father! Good morning Lord! You are the fountain of life. In You our essence is derived. We thank You for the privilege of standing in Your presence and worshipping at Your feet once again. Thank You for bringing us into union with Your son Jesus Christ. Thank You for bringing us into fellowship with Your Spirit.

PRAYERS OF DECLARATION

CP. No. 42

Heavenly Father! We lift up our eyes to You. Our help comes from You. You are our ever present help in times of need. You bestow glory on us and You lift up our heads. With Your help we can advance troops; with Your help we can scale any wall. You oh Lord are our advantage! You make up the difference in our lives. As we fellowship with Your Word today, we confess that it will take us beyond every limitation. This is our prayer in Jesus' name. Amen.

CP. No. 43

Oh Lord our God! Your name is Jehovah El-Shaddai. You are our all-sufficient God. Our sufficiency comes from You. You are able to make all grace abound to us. Today, we rest in Your Word that you have given us all that we need for life and godliness. You will not withhold any good thing from us. We declare that we shall receive all the supplies we need to fulfill our purposes in You. In Jesus' name. Amen.

CP. No. 44

Hallowed be Your name oh Lord our God. You have done great things for us. This is the day that You have made. Overwhelming gladness shall be our portion. Today is our day of rising! Our sorrows are being traded for joy. Our mouths shall be filled with laughter! As we encounter You today, we shall be built up once again, and our fortunes shall be restored. In Jesus name. Amen.

CP. No. 45

Our Father and our God! Thank You for the privilege of basking in the warmth of Your glorious presence. Thank You for uniting us all in Christ Jesus. We are no longer aliens. You have made us fellow citizens and members of Your family. As we fellowship with You and with one another, we receive empowerment to be solutions to our world. In Jesus' name we pray. Amen.

CP. No. 46

Thank You for creating us in Your image and making us to be "as you are" in this world. We are the salt of the earth and the light of the world; called to bring forth relevance and uncommon solutions to our world. From the fullness of your grace we have all received one blessing after another. No good thing will be withheld from us. All that you have given to us will come to us. This is our declaration In Jesus' name. Amen.

CP. No. 47

Oh Lord our God! How excellent is Your name in all the earth! Your glory fills the heaven like the waters cover the seas. This is the day that You have made. Overwhelming joy and incomprehensible peace shall be our por-

tion. As we fellowship with Your Word, it shall dispel every spell of darkness over our lives and cause us to be full of the excellent glory of God. In Jesus' name we pray.
Amen.

CP. No. 48

Our Father and our God! You are worthy to receive glory, honour and praise! You are the creator of everything. You are our everything. You have made known to us the path of life. We yield our spirits to be quickened by you this day, so that our lives can bring you the pleasure for which you created us. This is our confession in Jesus' name.
Amen.

CP. No. 49

Our hearts rejoice in You, O Lord our God! Great is Your faithfulness towards us. You have given us a crown of beauty for ashes. You gave us the oil of gladness for mourning. You have also given us the garment of praise for the spirit of heaviness. We shall be called trees of righteousness; the plantings of the Lord, ever bringing forth abiding fruits, to the glory of Your name. In Jesus' name.
Amen.

CP. No. 50

We lift up our eyes to You oh Lord! From the rising of the sun to the place where it sets, your name is to be praised. You are the bedrock of our success. Your Word is growing and prevailing in our lives. Your peace is

reigning supreme in our hearts. As we commune with You today, we shall experience Your metamorphic presence in the mighty name of Jesus.
Amen.

CP. No. 51

Heavenly Father! The God of all flesh! You reign supreme in our lives. You have given us dominion and power over life. You have made us a kingdom of kings and priests. Thank You for setting us among princes and causing us to ride upon the high places of life. Empower us today to yield to the force of Your wisdom, for by it we shall continue to reign and rule with Christ. In Jesus name we declare.
Amen.

CP. No. 52

Everlasting King of glory! Thank You for our privileges in Christ. You have called us into a life of abundance. We shall spread to the right and to the left. You have set us among princes to ride on the high places of life. You have made us blessings to our generation and vessels through which God's blessings flow. We declare that our eyes will be opened to enable us to always walk in this consciousness. In Jesus name.
Amen.

CP. No. 53

We worship You oh God, our King! You are our lot and our inheritance. The lots have fallen for us in pleasant places. You have given us a goodly heritage. You have made us a kingdom of kings and priests unto You, to rule and reign with You in life through Jesus Christ our Lord. Thank You for counting us faithful and empowering us to be effective co-labourers with You. We commit to a life of dominion and power today, In Jesus name. Amen.

PRAYERS OF PETITION AND SUPPLICATION

CP. No. 54

Our Lord and our God! We have come boldly to Your throne of grace this day. We have come to receive mercy and find grace for help in this time of need. As we worship You today with every sincerity of heart, may we receive strength afresh from You. Cause us to be made strong in our inner man and may Your strength be made perfect in our weaknesses, through Jesus Christ our Lord. Amen.

CP. No. 55

Hallowed be Your name oh Lord God. You are the Creator of the universe. None can be compared to You! As we encounter You today, cause us to ex- perience transformation in every way, so that we can in turn be blessings to our world in Jesus' name. Enable us to stand in your stead here on earth! This is our prayer in Jesus name. Amen.

CP. No. 56

Oh Lord our God, You who inhabits the praises of Your people. Let our wor- ship today come up as sweet incense unto You. Let the lifting of our hands be as the evening sacrifice. Make your presence known in our midst and may it be made manifest to bless, to heal, to transform, to prosper and to empower us today; in Jesus' name we pray. Amen.

CP. No. 57

Everlasting King of glory! We are here once again to worship You. You are the Fountain of life. In You our essence is derived. As we wait on You today, open our eyes and cause us to see that which we have not known. Cause our strength to be renewed, and may we soar on wings like the eagles, above every limitations in Jesus' name. Amen

CP. No. 58

To You oh Lord we lift up our hearts! You are great and you do marvellous deeds. As we fellowship with You today, May the entrance of Your Word illuminate our paths and cause us to walk in Your truth. Give us undivided hearts that we may fear Your name and be distinguished here on earth, to the glory of Your name; in Jesus' name we pray. Amen

CP. No. 59

Our dear Lord and Father! To You belong the lifting of our hands. Thank You for our heritage in You. As we fellowship with You today, cause us to grow more in grace and in the knowledge of our Lord and Saviour Jesus Christ. May the beauty of God in us be evidently manifest for all to see. May our lives be a picture of you. This we pray in Jesus' name.
Amen.

CP. No. 60

Our Lord and our God to whom all praise is due. We trust in Your holy name. May Your unfailing love rest upon us today even as we hope in You. Send forth Your words into our hearts that our lives will be transformed. May our worship open the floodgates of heaven and may we experience salvation as we hold our peace in Your presence. This is our prayer through Christ our Lord.
Amen.

CP. No. 61

Blessed be Your name O Lord of host. There is no God like You in heaven or on earth. Dominion and awe belong to You. You establish order in heaven and on earth. As we fellowship with You today, may the light of Your face shine upon us. Establish the work of our hands that we may be like trees planted by streams of waters. This is our prayer, in Jesus' name.
Amen

CP. No. 62

Forever Oh Lord, You are exalted above the heavens. Righteousness and justice are the foundation of Your throne. Satisfy us this day with Your unfailing love according to Your Word, that we may sing for joy and be glad all our days. Do great and awesome things in our midst and let Your name be magnified through Jesus Christ our Lord.
Amen.

CP. No. 63

Oh Lord our God. Breathe upon us Your Holy Spirit as we lift our hands and our lives in surrender to Your name today. Lead us today into an experience of Your love through the name of your son Jesus Christ. Our tongues will speak of Your righteousness and of Your praises today. As we worship you, may the words of our mouth and the meditations of our hearts be acceptable to You, through the Holy name of Your Son Jesus Christ.
Amen.

CP. No. 64

As we fellowship with You today oh Lord, may the rain of Your presence fall afresh on us; may your kingdom come in our lives; may Your Spirit cause our lives to align with Your ideal plan and purposes for us; May our lives increasingly reflect You and bring You glory; May Your perfect will be done in our lives. This we pray in Jesus' Name.
Amen.

CP. No. 65

Dear Lord. We have come once again to fellowship with You. You are the fountain of wisdom. Thank You for filling us with the Spirit of wisdom. As we fellowship with You today, help us to yield our spirit, soul and body to the force of Your wisdom; and may it keep moving us and guiding us in the path that You have ordained for us to walk, in Jesus' name.
Amen.

CP. No. 66

Eternal Rock of ages, we are here to worship You this day. As we worship, may the grace of our Lord Jesus be with us. Let the love of God dwell in our hearts and may the sweet fellowship of the Holy Spirit remain with us now and forever more, through Christ our Lord.
Amen

CP. No. 67

Oh Lord we have come before You to receive grace and mercy. May Your grace be poured on us abundantly along with faith and love that are in Christ Jesus. Cause our hearts to be stayed on You and show Yourself strong and mighty on our behalf. Holy Spirit, speak Your Word into our hearts and have Your way in our midst today. In Jesus' name we pray.
Amen.

CP. No. 68

Heavenly Father; Precious Lord! As we celebrate our love for You and for one another today, empower us to remain fruitful branches in You. May we not be castaways because of our unproductivity. Cause us to remain Your outstretched arm of salvation to our world. May we receive empowerment for influence and relevance once again today. This we ask through Jesus Christ our Lord.
Amen.

CP. No. 69

To You oh Lord we lift our hearts in worship. You deserve the glory and the honor. You alone are God. As we worship you today, cause our hearts to be opened that You may fill it with the treasures and wisdom of Your Word. May Your Word grow and prevail in our lives, over all circumstances. May we receive empowerment today for being a solution, by the force of Your wisdom. In Jesus name.
Amen.

CP. No. 70

Oh Lord our Heavenly Father, all the power and glory belong to You! We've come to worship at your feet. As we wait on You today with a sincere heart, may our light break forth like the dawn and may Your glory be our rearguard. Cause us to be strengthened by the power of Your Spirit that we may be able to mount up on wings as the eagles. Enable us to know You like never before that we might be energized us to do exploits for You. In Jesus' name.
Amen.

CP. No. 71

Gracious Lord! Giver of life! We marvel that You have created us in Your own image; each one part of Your plan, each one known, each one loved, and each one gifted. Make us strong in the power of Your spirit we pray, that our love may increasingly reflect Your own, and our lives may bring glory to You, whom we come to worship. Amen.

CP. No. 72

Everlasting King of glory! The Lord who reigns in majesty! You change time and seasons. Our times are in Your hands. As we commune with You today, open our eyes and cause us to see that which we have not known. Teach us from henceforth to number our days aright. Enable us to apply our hearts unto wisdom and may the entrance of Your Word switch us from simplicity to understanding, all the days of our lives in Jesus name. Amen.

CP. No. 73

Most Gracious God; hallowed by your name. May your name be honored today in all that we will say and do. May Your gracious presence surround us this day so that obedience to Your Word becomes a joy rather than a burden. May the depth of Your grace and the width of Your love, inspire us here and now. May we be empowered by Your Spirit today and forevermore, in Jesus' name we pray. Amen.

CP. No. 74

Almighty God! You are the Shepherd of our souls. We have come to tap into your unsearchable reservoir of supernatural resources. As we focus on You today, quieten our spirits to connect to You. May every hindrance to experiencing and manifesting Uncommon Solutions in us be eliminated by the power of Your Spirit. In Jesus' name we pray. Amen

CP. No. 75

Eternal Rock of Ages; the God of all creation. You are our firm foundation; the Author and Finisher of our faith. As we worship You today, enable us to strengthen our faith in You, that our lives will be more pleasing to You; and that we may enjoy Your favour even in the worst of times. May every pattern of unfruitful labour be destroyed in us, and may our lives be decorated with Your grace and favour. In Jesus' name. Amen!

CP. No. 76

Gracious Lord! We have come once again to behold the beauty of your presence. We have come to receive empowerment from your word. Help us to keep your lovely face ever before our eyes. Enable us to keep our minds perfectly stayed on your word. As we focus on your word today, may every distracting force be eliminated and may we be transformed into your likeness. In Jesus' name we pray. Amen.

CP. No. 77

Our Father and our God; You are Jehovah El-Gibbor; the man of war that fights our battles. As we encounter You today, may the red seas of our lives be parted; may every door of opportunity ordained for us be opened ; may your waves of favour surround us like a shield and cause us to walk in supernatural abundance; may goodness and mercy continually follow us and may we forever abide in your presence all the days of our lives. In Jesus' name. Amen.

CP. No. 78

Praise be to You oh Lord our God. You are the God who answers prayers; to You all men will come. We cast our cares at your feet this day. You will fulfill Your purposes for us. As we worship You today, may the Spirit of grace and supplication be poured upon us. Enable us like Zion, Esther, Daniel and Elijah of old to persist and travail in prayer, in order to prevail and birth our miracles. In Jesus' name we pray. Amen.

CP. No. 79

Everlasting King of Glory! We have come to worship You in Spirit and in truth. We have come to access the supernatural, mysterious and powerful highways that You have ordained for us. As we fellowship with You today, may every force acting against our progress be arrested now in Jesus name. May we contact a strong anointing for fervency in praying and fasting. This is our prayer in Jesus' name. Amen.

CP. No. 80

Great and Awesome God! The Creator and the Source of all life. Like a stream, may Your blessings flow through our lives to refresh and reinvigorate us. May Your Spirit be poured on us afresh that we might become part of Your never-ending stream. May He work in us and through us to make our lives colorful and spectacular indeed. This we pray in Jesus' name. Amen.

CP. No. 81

Oh Lord our heavenly Father! The God to whom all praise is due. You are our life. As we fellowship with You today, enable us to apply our hearts unto wisdom that Your will may be done in our lives. Empower us to take responsibility for our lives. May we receive the courage to keep advancing in the face of challenges. May the yoke of foolishness and laziness be destroyed in us, in Jesus name. Amen.

CP. No. 82

Gracious Lord! Thank You for Your steadfast love that is new every morning. Thank You for the gift of life. As we fellowship with You today, may we humbly accept Your Word that is planted and dwelling richly in us; may flesh be done away with in our lives; May every limitation to our metamorphosis be shattered by the power of Your spirit. As we submit our lives to the superiority of Your ways, may the light of Your knowledge flood our souls with uncommon solutions. In Jesus' name we pray. Amen.

PRAYERS OF PASSION, HUNGER, AND THIRST

CP. No. 83

Everlasting Father! Son of Righteousness! As we fellowship with You today, lead us into an experience of Your love. Saturate our hearts once again with Your steadfast love and in turn, make us conveyors of that pure and true love that has been shed abroad in our hearts by Your Spirit. May the rain of Your presence fall afresh on us. Reign in us oh Lord, today and forever more. In Jesus' name. Amen .

CP. No. 84

Our Father and our God, come and take Your holy place in our hearts. As we worship You today, may our lives be a picture of You. May it be a letter written by Your hand for the world to see and know that You live within us. Be the sole desire of our hearts. May all things become shadow in the light who You are. May the windows of heaven be opened and may the rain of Your presence fall afresh on us this day. This is our desire through Jesus Christ our Lord. Amen.

CP. No. 85

Precious Holy Spirit, we welcome You in our midst today. Take Your Holy place in our hearts. You are the centre of our joy. You are the air that we breathe. You are the essence of our lives. As we worship You today, birth in us a new fire and unquenchable passion for You. Fill us once again with the power of Your Spirit that we may become one with you. This is our prayer in Jesus name. Amen.

CP. No. 86

Oh Lord our God, from the rising of the sun to the place where it sets, we will forever seek Your face. We long to know You more. Only you can fill the longing of our hearts. Take us deeper in love with You. As we continually thirst and hunger for You, satisfy us with a revelation of who You are. May every root cause of spiritual barrenness in us be destroyed by Your anointing. This we pray in Jesus' name. Amen.

CP. No. 87

King of glory! King of peace! Awaken us this day to the glory of Your presence. Precious Holy Spirit, You are the fire in us. You are the power at work within us. As we fellowship with You today, shine through us that every darkness in us may be dispelled. Enable us to behold Your Word and be transformed by it. This is our prayer in Jesus name. Amen .

CP. No. 88

Precious Holy Spirit! You are the air that we breathe. You are the life that we live. You are our pearl of greatest prize. Your name is like perfumed poured out. You are the love of our lives! There is no greater joy than knowing You. As we fellowship with You today, show us Your face and let us hear Your voice; for Your face is beautiful and Your voice is sweet. Captivate our hearts once again and baptize us afresh with Your power. In Jesus name we pray.
Amen.

CP. No. 89

Sweet Holy Spirit! We lift up our eyes to you. Our help comes from You. You are the strength of our lives. You alone can still the raging storms in our lives. You alone can fill the yearnings of our hearts. You are our sole desire. No other love will compete with you. Your love is better than life. Saturate us with Your love today, that we may be drawn close to You. In Jesus' name we pray.
Amen.

CP. No. 90

Heavenly Father, Precious Lord! There is no other God beside You. We come humbly to You admitting our great need for You. You are our very life! Make Your presence known to us as we worship You. Enable us to behold You as You are. May every barrier to our transformation be destroyed in the mighty name of Jesus.
Amen.

PRAYERS OF CONSECRATION

CP. No. 91

Everlasting King of glory; You alone are worthy of our praise. You alone are holy. You alone are the Most High. We have come to bow before Your presence. As we fellowship with You today, help us to surrender our lives to You and turn from our own ways. Purify our hearts by the fire of Your presence so that we can fulfill Your purposes for us. May every weight that hinders our peace with You be destroyed and discarded. In Jesus' name.
Amen.

CP. No. 92

Our Father and our God! In You our hearts rejoice. We lift our hands and our lives in surrender to your name. We bless You for gracing us to stand in Your presence this day. Thank You for letting us see the light of Your countenance. You are the stronghold of our lives. As we worship today, may our worship come to You as a sweet smelling savour; May our lives be pleasing to You and may our focus on You be total. In Jesus name.
Amen.

CP. No. 93

Oh Lord our God, as we approach Your presence by the blood of Jesus Christ, may we draw near with a sincere heart in full assurance of faith. As we seek Your face today, may Your glory

be evident in our midst; May it cause every 'self' to die; May we live for You alone; May the entrapping of the world not have any more hold on us. Purge our hearts today and cause us to be subject to the leadership of the Holy Spirit, through Jesus Christ our Lord.
Amen.

PRAYERS OF GRATITUDE AND THANKSGIVING

CP. No. 94

We thank You oh God for the dawning of a new day. Thank You for the newness of this day's mercies. Great is Your faithfulness towards us oh Lord. Thank You for bringing us into Your presence. In Your presence there is fullness of joy. At Your right hand are pleasures forever more. Thank You for loving us with such great and everlasting love. Help us to understand the breadth, length, height and depth of Your love for us. This we pray in Jesus' name.
Amen.

CP. No. 95

We will sing this day of Your steadfast love. We will glorify Your name forever. Great is Your love towards us. You have been our fortress and our refuge in times of trouble. You have

delivered us from the depths of the grave. You have preserved our lives. We will sing of Your great love forever, and with our mouths make Your faithfulness known through all generations. In Jesus name.
Amen.

CP. No. 96

Glory to You oh God, now and forever more! We bless You for the marvellous gift of Your life. Thank You for giving us everything we need for life and godliness. Our lives are expressions of Your endless possibilities. Thank You for prospering us and causing us to experience the manifestation of Your infinite blessings. Give us the understanding to know that we are blessed to be blessings. To You be all the glory, in Jesus' name.
Amen.

CP. No. 97

Heavenly Father we appreciate You today! Thank You for G-R-A-C-E; God's Riches At Christ's Expense! We bless You for the sweet fellowship and union that You have brought us into by the blood of Jesus Christ. Thank You for making us blameless, irreproachable and acceptable in Your sight.Help us to love You more! In Jesus' name.
Amen.

CP. No. 98

Everlasting King of glory! Thank You for our privileges in Christ. We thank You for bringing us into our season of abundance. We shall spread to the right and to the left. You have set us

among princes to ride on the high
places of life. Thank You for making
us blessings to our generation and
vessels through which God's blessings
flow. Help us to always walk in this
consciousness. In Jesus name.
Amen.

Get this Classic Spiritual Resource from
Rev. Wildfire D-Favour

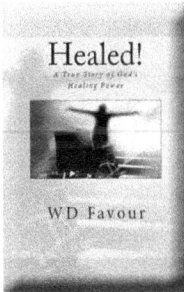

HEALED!

A True Story of God's
Healing Power

After 17 years of pain, agony, uncertainties, fear,
and depression due to debilitating illnesses, Wildfire
D-Favour experienced the miracle of divine healing.

This booklet not only tells that amazing story, it also challenges you to trust God
for your healing and that of your loved ones.

The message of this booklet is simple - you too can be HEALED!

Available at all Citizens Family Church Offices

HYMNS AND SPIRITUAL SONGS

"Let the word of Christ dwell in you richly as you teach and admonish one another with all wisdom, and as you sing psalms, hymns and spiritual songs with gratitude in your hearts to God." ~
Colossians 3:16

Praise, and Thanksgiving

HSS 1

1. Praise my soul the King of heaven;
To His feet thy tribute bring;
Ransomed, healed, restored, forgiven,
Who like thee His praise shall sing?
Praise Him! Praise Him!
Praise the everlasting King!

2. Praise Him for His grace and favour
To our fathers in distress;
Praise Him, still the same as ever,
Slow to chide, and swift to bless:
Praise Him! Praise Him!
Glorious in His faithfulness!

3. Father like He tends and spares us,
Well our feeble frame He knows;
In His hands He gently bears us,
Rescues us from all our foes;
Praise Him! Praise Him!
Widely as His mercies flows.

4. Angels, help us to adore Him,
Ye behold Him face to face!
Sun and moon, bow down before Him!
Dwellers all in time and space,
Praise Him! Praise Him!
Praise with us the God of grace!

Amen.

HSS 2

1. A safe stronghold our God is still,
A trusty shield and weapon
He'll keep us clear from all the ill
That hath now o'er taken
The ancient prince of hell,
Hath risen with purpose fell
Strong mail of craft and power,
He ruleth in this hour
On earth is not his fellow

2. With force of arms we nothing can
Full soon were we down-ridden
But for us fights the proper Man
Who, God Himself hath bidden
Ask ye, who is this same?
Christ Jesus is His name
The Lord Sabaoth's Son,
He and no other one
Shall conquer in the battle

3. God's Word for all their craft and force
One moment will not linger
But, spite of hell shall have its course;
'Tis written by His finger
And though they take our life,
Goods, honor, children, wife
Yet is their profit small,
These things shall vanish all
The city of God remaineth.

Amen.

HSS 3

1. Thou whose Almighty Word
Chaos and darkness heard
And took their flight
Hear us we humbly pray
And where the Gospel day
Sheds not its glorious ray
Let there be light!

2. Thou who didst come to bring
On Thy redeeming wing
Healing and sight
Health to the sick in mind
Sight to the inly blind
Oh now to all mankind
Let there be light!

3. Spirit of truth and love
Life-giving, Holy Dove
Speed forth Thy flight!
Move on the water's face
By Thy Almighty grace
And in earth's darkest place
Let there be light!

4. Holy and Blessed Three
   Glorious Trinity
   Wisdom, Love, Might!
   Boundless as ocean's tide
   Rolling in fullest pride
   O'er the world far and wide
   Let there be light!

Amen

HSS 4

1. Come Thou Almighty King
   Help us Thy name to sing
   Help us to praise
   Father all glorious
   O'er all victorious
   Come and reign over us
   Ancient of days!

2. Come Thou incarnate Word
   Gird on Thy mighty Word
   Our prayer attend
   Come and Thy people bless
   And give Thy Word success
   Spirit of holiness
   On us descend!

3. Come Holy Comforter
   Thy sacred witness bear
   In this glad hour
   Thou who Almighty art
   Now rule in every heart
   And ne'er from us depart
   Spirit of power!

4. To the Great One in Three
   The highest praises be
   Hence evermore
   His Sovereign Majesty
   May we in glory see
   And to eternity
   Love and adore

Amen

HSS 5

1. All people that on earth do dwell
   Sing to the Lord with cheerful voice
   Him serve with fear, His praise forth tell
   Come ye before Him and rejoice

2. Know that the Lord is God indeed
   Without our aid He did us make
   We are His flock, He doth us feed
   And for His sheep He doth us take

3. Oh, enter then His gates with praise
   Approach with joy His courts unto
   Praise, loud and bless His name always
   For it is seemly so to do

4. For why? the Lord our God is good
   His mercy is forever sure
   His truth at all times firmly stood
   And shall from age to age endure

Amen

HSS 6

1. Oh , worship the King, All glorious above
   Oh, gratefully sing, His power and His love;
   Our Shield and Defender, the Ancient of Days,
   Pavilioned in splendor, and Girded with praise..

2. Oh tell of His might, Oh, sing of His grace!
   Whose robe is the light, whose canopy space;
   His chariots of wrath, the deep thunder clouds form
   And dark is Hs path on the wings of the storm.

3. Thy bountiful care, what tongue can recite?
   It breathes in the air, it shines in the light;
   It streams from the hills, it descends to the plain,
   And sweetly distills in the dew and the rain.

4. O measureless Might! Ineffable love!
   While angels delight, to hymn Thee above,
   Thy humbler creation, though feeble their lays,
   With true adoration, shall sing to Thy praise.
   Amen

HSS 7

1. Oh praise ye the Lord, with heart and
with voice
His mercies record, and round Him
rejoice
Ye children of Zion, Your Saviour adore
And learn to rely on, His grace
evermore

2. Repose on His arm, Ye sheep of His fold
What terror can harm, with Him to
uphold
His saints are His treasure, their peace
will He seek
And pour without measure, His gifts on
the meek

3. Go on in His might, ye men of the Lord
His Word be your light, His promise
Your sword
The King of salvation, Your foes will
subdue
Bring forth your oblation, your praises
renew

Amen

HSS 8

1. Holy, Holy, Holy! Lord God Almighty!
Early in the morning our song shall rise
to Thee;
Holy, Holy, Holy! Merciful and mighty!
God in three Persons, blessed Trinity!

2. Holy, Holy, Holy! All the saints adore
Thee,
Casting down their golden crowns
around the glassy sea;
Cherubim and seraphim falling down
before Thee,
Which wert and art and evermore shalt
be.

3. Holy! Holy! Holy! Though the darkness
hide Thee,
Though the eye of sinful man thy glory
may not see,
Only Thou art holy, there is none beside
Thee
Perfect in power, in love, and purity.

4. Holy, Holy, Holy! Lord God Almighty!
All Thy works shall praise Thy name in
earth and sky and sea;
Holy, Holy, Holy! Merciful and mighty!
God in three Persons, blessed Trinity!

Amen

HSS 9

1. To God be the glory! Great things He
hath done
So loved He the world that He gave us
His Son;
Who yielded His life an atonement for
sin,
And opened the Life-gate that all may
go in.

Praise the Lord! Praise the Lord!
Let the earth hear His voice!
Praise the Lord! Praise The Lord!
Let the people rejoice!
Oh, come to the Father through Jesus
the Son;
And give Him the glory, great things He
hath done!

2. O perfect redemption, the purchase of
blood,
To every believer the promise of God;
The vilest offender who truly believes,
That moment from Jesus a pardon
receives.

3. Great things He hath taught us, great
things He hath done,
And great our rejoicing through Jesus
the Son;
But purer, and higher and greater will
be
Our wonder, our rapture when Jesus
we see.

Amen

HSS 10

1. Who is He in yonder stall?
At His feet the shepherds fall?

'Tis the Lord, oh wondrous story
'Tis the Lord, the King of glory
At His feet, we humbly fall
Crown Him! Crown Him Lord of all!

2. Who is He in deep distress
   Fasting in the wilderness?

3. Who is He, to Whom they bring
   All the sick and sorrowing

4. Who is He, the gathering throng
   Greet with loud triumphant song

5. Lo, at midnight who is He
   Prays in dark Gethsemane

6. Who is He, on yonder tree
   Dies in grief and agony

7. Who is He, who from the grave
   Comes to succour, help and save

8. Who is He, who from His throne
   Rules through all the worlds alone

   Amen

HSS 11

1. My God how wonderful thou art
   Thy majesty how bright
   How beautiful, Thy mercy-seat
   In depths of burning light

2. How dread are Thine eternal years
   O everlasting Lord
   By prostrate spirits, day and night
   Incessantly adore

3. How wonderful, how beautiful
   The sight of Thee must be
   Thine endless wisdom, boundless
   power
   And aweful purity

4. Oh how I fear Thee Living God
   With deepest, tenderest fears
   And worship Thee with trembling hope
   And penitential tears

5. Yet I may love Thee too oh Lord
   Almighty as thou art
   For Thou hast stooped to ask of me
   The love of my poor heart

6. No earthly father loves like Thee
   No mother e'er so mild
   Bears and forbears, as Thou hast done
   With me Thy sinful child

7. Father of Jesus, love's reward
   What rapture will it be
   Prostrate before Thy throne to lie
   And gaze and gaze on Thee!

   Amen

HSS 12

1. How sweet the name of Jesus sounds
   In a believer's ear
   It soothes his sorrows
   Heals his wounds
   And drives away his fear

2. It makes the wounded spirit whole
   And calms the troubled breast
   'Tis manna to the hungry soul
   And to the weary rest

3. Dear name the Rock on which I build
   My shield and hiding-place
   My never-failing treasury filled
   With boundless stores of grace

4. Jesus, my Shepherd, Brother, Friend
   My Prophet, Priest and King
   My Lord, My Way, my life, my End
   Accept the praise I bring

   Amen

HSS 13

1. All hail the power of JESUS NAME!
   Let angels prostrate fall;
   Bring forth the royal diadem,
   And crown Him, Lord of all!

2. Crown Him, ye martyrs of our God,
   Who from His altar call;
   Extol the stem of Jesse's rod,
   And crown Him Lord of all

3. Ye chosen seed of Israel's race
   A remnant weak and small,
   Hail Him who saves you by His grace,
   And crown Him Lord of all!

4. Ye gentile sinners, ne'er forget
   The wormwood and the gall;
   Go spread your trophies at His feet,
   And crown Him Lord of all!

5. Let every kindred, every tribe,
   On this terrestrial ball,
   To Him all majesty ascribe,
   And crown Him Lord of all!

6. Oh that with yonder sacred throng
   We at His feet may fall;
   Join in the everlasting song,
   And crown Him, Lord of all

   Amen

HSS 14

1. Be glad in the Lord and rejoice,
   All ye that are upright in heart;
   And ye that have made Him your choice,
   Bid sadness and sorrow depart.

   Rejoice!... Rejoice !...
   Be glad in the Lord and rejoice!...

2. Be joyful, for He is the Lord,
   On earth and in heaven supreme;
   He fashions and rules by His Word;
   The "Mighty" and "Strong" to redeem.

3. What though in the conflict for right.
   Your enemies almost prevail!
   God's armies, just hid from your sight,
   Are more than the foes which assail.

4. Though darkness surround you by day,
   Your sky by the night be o'er cast,
   Let nothing your spirit dismay,
   But trust till the danger is past.

5. Be glad in the Lord and rejoice,
   His praises proclaiming in song;
   With harp, and with organ and voice,
   The loud hallelujah prolong!

   Amen

HSS 15

1. Oh for a thousand tongues to sing
   My great Redeemer's praise;
   The glories of my God and King,
   The triumphs of His grace...

2. My gracious Master and my God
   Assist me to proclaim
   To spread thro' all the earth abroad
   The honors of Thy name...

3. Jesus, the Name that charms our fears,
   That bids our sorrows cease;
   'Tis music in the sinner's ears,
   'Tis life, and health, and peace...

4. He breaks the power of cancelled sin,
   He sets the prisoner free;
   His blood can make the foulest clean'
   His blood avails for me
   Amen.

HSS 16

1. Rejoice the Lord is King
   Your God and King adore
   Mortals give thanks and sing
   And triumph evermore
   Lift up your heart, lift up your voice
   Rejoice again, ye saints rejoice

2. Rejoice the Saviour Reigns
   The God of truth and love
   When He had purged our stains
   He took His seat above
   Lift up your heart, lift up......

3. His Kingdom cannot fail
   He rules o'er earth and heaven
   The keys of death and hell
   Are to our Jesus given
   Lift up your heart, lift up...........

4. He sits at God's right hand
   Till all HIs foes submit
   And bow to His command
   And fall beneath His feet
   Lift up your heart, lift up............

   Amen.

HSS 17

1. Songs of praise the angels sang,
Heaven with hallelujah rang,
When Jehovah's work begun,
When He spake and it was done

2. Songs of praise awoke the morn,
When the Prince of peace was born,
Songs of praise arose when He
Captive led captivity.

3. Heaven and earth must pass away,
Songs of praise shall crown that day,
God will make new heavens and earth,
Songs of praise shall hail their birth.

4. And will man alone be dumb,
Till that glorious Kingdom come?
No; the Church delights to raise;
Psalms and hymns, and songs of praise.

5. Saints below, with heart and voice
Still in songs of praise rejoice;
Learning here by faith and love'
Songs of praise to sing above

6. Borne upon their latest breath
Songs of praise shall conquer death;
Then, amidst eternal joy,
Songs of praise their powers employ.
Amen.

HSS 18

1. Hallelujah! Hallelujah
Hearts to heaven and voices raise
Sing to God a hymn of gladness
Sing to God a hymn of praise
He who on the cross a victim
For the world's salvation bled
Jesus Christ the King of glory
Now is risen from the dead

2. Christ is risen, Christ the first-fruit
Of the holy harvest field
Which will all its full abundance
At His glorious advent yield
Then the golden ears of harvest
Will their heads before Him wave
Ripened by His glorious sunshine
From the furrows of the grave

3. Hallelujah! Hallelujah!
Glory be to God on high
Hallelujah to the Saviour
Who has gained the victory
Hallelujah to the Spirit
Let our high ascriptions be
Hallelujah! Now and ever
To the Blessed Trinity

Amen.

HSS 19

1. Glorious things of thee are spoken
Zion city of our God
He whose Word cannot be broken
Formed thee for His own abode
On the Rock of ages founded
What can shake thy sure repose
With salvation's walls surrounded
Thou mays't smile at all thy foes

2. See the streams of living waters
Springing from eternal love
Well supply thy sons and daughters
And all fear of want remove
Who can faint while such a river
Ever flows their thirst to assuage
Grace, which like the Lord the Giver
Never fails from age to age

3. Round each habitation hovering
See the cloud and fire appear
For a glory and a covering
Showing that the Lord is near
He who gives them daily manna
He who listens when they cry
Let him hear the loud hosanna
Rising to His throne on high
Amen

HSS 20

1. Low in the grave He lay
Jesus, my Saviour
Waiting the coming day
Jesus my Lord!

Up from the grace He arose
With a mighty triumph o'er His foes
He arose a victor from the dark domain
And He lives forever with the saints to
reign
He arose! He arose!
Hallelujah! Christ arose!

2. Vainly they watch His bed
Jesus, my Saviour!
Vainly they seal the dead
Jesus my Lord!

3. Death cannot keep His prey
Jesus, my Saviour
He tore the bars away
Jesus my Lord!

Amen

HSS 21

1. Let us with a gladsome mind
Praise the Lord for He is kind
For His mercies ay endure
Ever faithful, ever sure

2. Let us blaze His name abroad
For of gods, he is the God
For His mercies, etc.

3. He with all-commanding might
Filled the new made world with light
For His mercies, etc.

4. He the golden-tressed sun
Caused all day His course to run
For His mercies, etc.

5. And the horned moon at night
'Mid her spangled sister's bright
For His mercies, etc.

6. All things living, He doth feed
His full hand supplies their need
For His mercies, etc.

Amen

HSS 22

1. What a friend we have in Jesus
All our sins and griefs to bear!
What a privilege to carry,
Everything to God in prayer.
Oh, what peace we often forfeit,
Oh, what needless pain we bear
All because we do not carry
Everything to God in prayer!

2. Have we trials and temptations?
Is there trouble anywhere?
We should never be discouraged;
Take it to the Lord in prayer.
Can we find a friend so Faithful,
Who will all our sorrows share?
Jesus knows our every weakness
Take it to the Lord in prayer.

3. Are we weak and heavy-laden,
Cumbered with a load of care?
Precious Savior, still our refuge
Take it to the Lord in prayer.
Do thy friends despise, forsake thee?
Take it to the Lord in prayer;
In His arms, He'll take and shield thee.
Thou wilt find a solace there.

Amen

HSS 23

1. The Church is one foundation
Is Jesus Christ her Lord
She is His new creation
By Water and the Word
From heaven He came and sought her
To be His holy bride
With His own blood He bought her
And for her life He died

2. Elect from ever nation
Yet one o'er all the earth
Her charter of salvation
One Lord, one Faith, one birth
One Holy name she blesses
Partakes one holy food
And to one hope she presses
With every grace endued

3. Yet she on earth hath union
With God the Three in One
And mystic sweet communion
With those whose rest is won
Oh happy ones and holy!
Lord give us grace that we
Like them, the meek and lowly
On high may dwell with Thee

Amen

HSS 24

1. Father of mercies in Thy Word
   What endless glory shines
   Forever be Thy name adored
   For these celestial lines

2. Here may the wretched sons of want
   Exhaustless riches find
   Riches above what earth can grant
   And lasting as the mind

3. Hear the Redeemer's welcome voice
   Spreads heavenly peace around
   And life and everlasting joys
   Attend the blissful sound

4. Oh may these heavenly pages be
   My ever dear delight
   And still new beauties may I see
   And still increasing light

5. Divine Instructor, gracious Lord
   Be Thou forever near
   Teach me to love Thy sacred Word
   And view my Saviour there

   Amen

HSS 25

1. The King of love, my Shepherd is
   Whose goodness faileth never
   I nothing lack if I am His
   And He is mine forever

2. Where streams of living water flow
   My ransomed soul He leadeth
   And where the verdant pastures grow
   With food celestial feedeth

3. Perverse and foolish oft I strayed
   But yet in love He sought me
   And on His shoulder gently laid
   And home rejoicing brought me

4. In death's dark vale, I fear no ill
   With Thee dear Lord beside me
   Thy rod and staff, my comfort still
   Thy cross before to guide me

5. And so through all the length of days
   Thy goodness faileth never
   Good Shepherd my I sing Thy praise
   Within Thy house forever

   Amen

HSS 26

1. Jesus shall reign where'er the sun
   Doth His successive journeys run;
   His kingdom stretch from shore to shore,
   Till moons shall wax and wane no more.

2. Peoples and realms from every tongue
   Dwell on His love with sweetest song;
   And infant voices shall proclaim
   Their early blessings on His name.

3. To Him shall endless prayers be made,
   And endless praises crown His head;
   His name like sweet perfume shall rise,
   With every morning sacrifice.

4. Then all the earth shall rise and bring
   Peculiar honors to the King;
   Angels descend with songs again,
   And earth repeat the loud Amen

   Amen

HSS 27

1. At the name of Jesus,
   Every knee shall bow
   Every tongue confess Him,
   King of glory now
   'Tis the Father's pleasure,
   We should call Him Lord
   Who from the beginning,
   Was the living Word

2. At His voice creation,
   Sprang at once to sight
   All the angel faces,
   All the hosts of light
   Throne and dominations,
   Stars upon their way
   All the heavenly orders,
   In their great array

3. Humbled for a season,
   To receive a name
   From the lips of sinners,
   Unto whom He came
   Faithfully He bore it,
   Spotless to the last
   Brought it back victorious,
   When from death He passed

   Amen

HSS 28

1. Stand up and bless the LORD
   Ye people of His choice
   Stand up and bless the Lord your God
   With heart and soul and voice

2. Though high above all praise
   Above all blessing high
   Who would not fear His Holy name
   And loud and magnify

3. O for the living flame
   From His own altar brought
   To touch our lips, our minds inspire
   And wing to heaven our thought

4. God is our strength and song
   And His salvation ours
   Then be His love in Christ proclaimed
   With all our ransomed powers

5. Stand up and bless the Lord
   The Lord your God adore
   Stand up and bless His glorious name
   Henceforth forevermore

   Amen

HSS 29

1. Immortal, Invisible, God Only Wise,
   In light inaccessible hid from our eyes,
   Most blessed, most glorious, the
   Ancient of Days,
   Almighty, Victorious, Thy great name
   we praise.

2. Unresting, unhasting and silent as light,
   Nor wanting, nor wasting, thou rulest
   in might;
   Thy justice like mountains high soaring
   above
   Thy clouds which are fountains of
   goodness and love.

3. To all life Thou givest, to both great and
   small;
   In all life Thou livest, the true life of all;
   We blossom we flourish as leaves on
   the tree,
   And wither and perish; but naught
   changeth Thee.

4. Great Father of glory, pure Father of
   light,
   Thine angels adore Thee, all veiling
   their sight;
   All laud we would render: oh help us
   to see
   'Tis only the splendor of light hideth
   Thee.
   Amen

HSS 30

1. NOW thank we all our God,
   With hearts and hands and voices,
   Who wondrous things hath done,
   In whom His world rejoices;
   Who from our mother's arms
   Hath blessed us on our way
   With countless gifts of love,
   And still is our today.

2. O may this bounteous God
   Through all our life be near us
   With ever joyful hearts
   And blessed peace to cheer us;
   And keep us in His grace,
   And guide us when perplexed,
   And free us from all ills
   In this world and the next.

3. All praise and thanks to God
   The Father now be given,
   The Son and Him who reigns
   With them in highest heaven,
   The One eternal God,
   Whom earth and heaven adore,
   For thus it was, is now,
   And shall be evermore.

   Amen

HSS 31

1. PRAISE to the Lord, the Almighty, the
   King of creation;
   O my soul, praise Him for He is thy
   health and salvation:
   All ye who hear,
   Now to His temple draw near,
   Joining in glad adoration.

2. PRAISE to the Lord, who o'er all things
   so wondrously reigneth,
   Shieldeth thee gently from harm, or
   when fainting sustaineth:
   Hast thou not seen_
   How thy heart's wishes have been_
   Granted in what He ordaineth?

3. PRAISE to the Lord, who doth prosper
   thy work and defend thee;
   Surely His goodness and mercy shall
   daily attend thee.
   Ponder anew
   What the Almighty can do,
   If to the end He befriend thee.

4. PRAISE to the Lord, O let all that is in
   me adore Him!
   All that hath life and breath come now
   with praises before Him!
   Let the Amen
   Sound from His people again:
   Gladly for ay we adore Him.

   Amen

HSS 32

1. We plough the fields and scatter,
   The good seed on the land;
   But it is fed and watered
   By God's Almighty hand:
   He sends the snow in winter,
   The warmth to swell the grain;
   The breezes, and the sunshine,
   And soft refreshing rain.

   All good gifts around us
   Are sent from heaven above;
   Then thank the Lord, oh, thank the Lord,
   For all His love!

2. He only is the Maker
   Of all things near and far:
   He paints the wayside flower;
   He lights the evening star;
   The winds and waves obey Him;
   By Him the birds are fed;
   Much more to us His children,
   He gives our daily bread.

3. We thank Thee then, oh Father,
   For all things bright and good:
   The seed-time and the harvest,
   Our life, our health, our food.
   Accept the gifts we offer
   For all Thy love imparts;
   And- what Thou most desirest-
   Our humble, thankful hearts.

   Amen

HSS 33

1. Great is Thy faithfulness, Oh God my
   Father,
   There is no shadow of turning with
   Thee,
   Thou changest not, Thy compassion
   they fail not.
   As Thou hast been, Thou forever will be.

   Great is Thy faith fullness, great is Thy
   faithfulness.
   Morning by morning new mercies I see,
   All I have needed Thy hands hath
   provided.
   Great is Thy faithfulness, Lord unto me.

2. Summer and winter, spring-time and
   harvest
   Sun, moon and stars in their courses
   above
   Join with all angels in manifold witness
   To Thy great faithfulness, mercy and
   love

3. Pardon for sin and a peace that
   endureth
   Thine own dear presence cheer and to
   guide
   Strength for today and bright hopes for
   tomorrow
   Blessings all mine with ten thousand
   beside
   Amen

HSS 34

1. God moves in a mysterious way
   His wonders to perform;
   He plants His footsteps in the sea,
   And rides upon the storm.

2. Deep in unfathomable mines
   Of never-failing skill
   He treasures up His bright designs,
   And works His sovereign will.

3. Ye fearful saints, fresh courage take!
   The clouds ye so much dread
   Are big with mercy, and will break
   In blessings on your head.

4. Judge not the Lord by feeble sense
   But trust Him for His grace;
   Behind a frowning providence
   He hides a smiling face

5. His purposes will ripen fast,
   Unfolding every hour;
   The bud may have a bitter taste,
   But sweet will be the flower.

6. Blind unbelief is sure to err'
   And scan His work in vain;
   God is His own interpreter,
   And He will make it plain….

   Amen

HSS 35

1. O Lord my God, when I in awesome
   wonder
   Consider all the works Thy Hands hath
   made
   I see the stars, I hear the rolling thunder
   Thy power throughout the universe
   display.

   *Then sings my soul, my Savior God to
   Thee*
   *How great Thou art, how great Thou
   art…*
   *Then sings my soul, my Savior God to
   Thee;*
   *How great Thou art, how great Thou
   art!*

2. When through the woods and forest
   glades I wonder,
   I hear the birds sing sweetly in the trees
   When I look down from lofty mountain
   grandeur
   And hear the brook and feel the gentle
   breeze.

3. But when I think, that God His son not
   sparing'
   Sent Him to die, I scarce can take it in.
   That on the cross, my burden gladly
   bearing,
   He bled and died to take away my sin.

4. When Christ shall come with shouts of
   acclamation,
   And claim His own, what joy shall fill my
   heart.
   Then I shall bow in humble adoration,
   And there proclaim, My God, how great
   Thou art!

   Amen

HSS 36

1. Alleluia, sing to Jesus!
   His the scepter, His the throne
   Alleluia! His the triumph,
   His the victory alone
   Hark! The songs of peaceful sion;
   Thunder like a mighty flood
   Jesus out of every nation,
   Hath redeemed us by His blood

2. Alleluia! Not as orphans,
   Are we left in sorrow now
   Alleluia! He is near us,
   Faith believes nor questions now
   Though the cloud from sight received
   Him
   When the forty days were o'er
   Shall our hearts forget His promise;
   "I am with you ever more"

3. Alleluia! Bread of angels,
   Thou on earth our food, our stay
   Alleluia! Here the sinful,
   Flee to Thee from day to day
   Intercessor, friend of sinners,
   Earth's Redeemer, plead for me
   When the songs of all the sinless,
   Sweep across the crystal sea.

   Amen

HSS 37

1. The Lord's my Shepherd, I'll not want;
He makes me down to lie
In pastures green, He leadeth me
The quiet waters by.

2. My soul He doth restore again;
And me to walk doth make
Within the paths of righteousness,
Ev'n for His own name's sake

3. Yea, though I walk in death's dark vale,
Yet will I fear none ill;
For Thou art with me; and Thy rod
And staff me comfort still.

4. My table Thou hast furnished
In presence of my foes;
My head Thou dost with oil anoint'
My cup overflows.

5. Goodness and mercy all my life
Shall surely follow me;
And in God's house for evermore
My dwelling place shall be.

Amen

HSS 38

1. Lord Thy Word abideth
And our footsteps guideth
Who its truth believeth
Light and joy receiveth

2. When our foes are near us
Then Thy Word doth cheer us
Word of consolation
Message of salvation

3. Word of mercy giving
Succour to the living
Word of life supplying
Comfort to the dying

4. O that we discerning
Its most holy learning
Lord may love and fear Thee
Evermore be near Thee

Amen

HSS 39

1. New every morning is the love
Our wakening and uprising prove;
Through sleep and darkness safely
brought
Restored to life and power and thought.

2. New mercies, each returning day,
Hover around us while we pray;
New perils past, new sins forgiven,
New thoughts of God, new hopes of
heaven.

3. If on our daily course our mind
Be set to hallow all we find,
New treasures still, of countless price,
God will provide for sacrifice.

4. The trivial round, the common task,
Will furnish all we need to ask,
Room to deny ourselves a road
To bring us daily nearer God.

5. Only, O Lord in Thy dear love
Fit us for perfect rest above;
And help us, this and every day,
To live more nearly as we pray.

Amen

HSS 40

1. Lo He comes with clouds descending
Once for favoured sinner's slain
Thousand thousand saints attending
Swell the triumph of His train
Alleluia! Alleluia! Alleluia!
Christ appears on earth to reign

2. Every eye shall now behold Him
Robed in dreadful majesty
Those who set at naught and sold Him
Pierced and nailed Him to the tree
Deeply Wailing, deeply ...... etc
Shall the true Messiah see

3. Those dear tokens of His Passion
Still His dazzling body bears
Cause of endless exultation
To His ransomed worshipers
With what rapture, ...etc.
Gaze we on those glorious scars

4. Yea, Amen let all adore Thee
   High on Thine eternal throne
   Saviour, take the power and glory
   Claim the kingdom for Thine own
   Alleluia! Alleluia! etc.
   Thou shalt reign and Thou alone

   Amen

HSS 41

1. Praise the Lord! ye heavens adore Him
   Praise Him angels in the height
   Sun and moon rejoice before Him
   Praise Him all ye stars and light
   Praise the Lord! For He has spoken
   Worlds His mighty voice obeyed
   Laws which never shall be broken
   For their guidance He hath made

2. Praise the Lord, for He is glorious
   Never shall His promise fail
   God hath made His saints victorious
   Sin and death shall not prevail
   Praise the God of our salvation
   Hosts on high, His power proclaim
   Heaven and earth and all creation
   Laud and magnify His name

   Amen

HSS 42

1. Pleasant are Thy courts above
   In the land of light and love
   Pleasant are Thy courts below
   In this land of sin and woe
   O, my spirit longs and faints
   For the converse of Thy saints
   For the brightness of Thy face
   For Thy fullness, God of grace

2. Happy birds that sing and fly
   Round Thy altars, o most High
   Happier souls that find a rest
   In a heavenly Father's breast
   Like the wandering dove that found
   No repose on earth around
   They can to their ark repair
   And enjoy it ever there

3. Happy souls their praises flow
   Even in this vale of woe
   Waters in the desert rise
   Manna feeds them from the skies
   On they go from strength to strength
   Till they reach Thy throne at length
   At Thy feet adoring fall
   Who hast led them safe through all

   Amen

HSS 43

1. Ye servants of God, your Master
   proclaim
   And publish abroad, His wonderful
   name
   The name all-victorious of Jesus extol
   His Kingdom is glorious and rules over
   all

2. God ruleth on high, Almighty to save
   And still He is nigh, his presence we
   have
   The great congregation His triumph
   shall sing
   Ascribing salvation to Jesus our King

3. Salvation to God, who sits on the
   throne
   Let all cry aloud, and honor the Son
   The praises of Jesus and angels
   proclaim
   Fall down on their faces and worship
   the Lamb

4. Then let us adore, and give Him His
   right
   All glory and power, all wisdom and
   might
   And honor and blessing, with angels
   above
   And thanks never-ceasing, and infinite
   love

   Amen

PENITENCE
AND INTERCESSION

HSS 44

1. Holy Words, Long preserved
   For our walk in this world
   May resound, with God's own heart,
   O let the ancient Words impart.

   Ancient Words, Ever true
   Changing me, and changing you,
   We have come with open hearts
   O let the Ancient Words impart

2. Words of life, Words of hope,
   Give us strength, help us grow,
   In this world where'er we roll,
   Ancient Words will guide us home.

3. Holy Words, of our faith,
   Handed down, to this age
   Came to us, through sacrifice
   O heed the faithful Words of Christ.

4. Holy Words, long preserved,
   For our walk, in this world,
   May resound, with God's own heart,
   O let the ancient Words impart.

   Amen

HSS 45

1. Spirit Divine! Attend our prayers,
   And make our hearts Thy home;
   Descend with all Thy gracious powers
   Oh come, great Spirit , come!

2. Come as the light, to us reveal
   Our emptiness and woe;
   And lead us in those paths of life
   Where all the righteous go.

3. Come as the fire and purge our hearts,
   Like sacrificial flame;
   Let our whole soul, an offering be
   To our Redeemer's name.

4. Come as the dew, and sweetly bless
   This consecrated hour;
   May barrenness rejoice to own
   Thy fertilizing power.

5. Come as the wind with rushing sound
   And Pentecostal grace;
   That all of woman born may see
   The glory of Thy face.
   Amen

HSS 46

1. Lord, dismiss us with Thy blessing,
   Fill our hearts with joy and peace;
   Let us each, Thy love possessing,
   Triumph in redeeming grace.
   Oh, refresh us, oh, refresh us.
   Travelling through this wilderness.

2. Thanks we give, and adoration,
   For Thy gospel's joyful sound;
   May the fruits of Thy salvation
   In our hearts and lives abound.
   Ever faithful, ever faithful
   To the truth may we be found.

3. So, when'er the signal's given
   Us from earth to call away.
   Borne on angel's wings to heaven,
   Glad the summons to obey,
   May we ever, may we ever,
   Reign with Christ in endless day.

   Amen

HSS 47

1. Hark my soul! It is the Lord
   'Tis Thy Saviour hear His Word
   Jesus speaks and speaks to thee
   Say poor sinner, lov'st Thou me

2. I delivered thee when bound
   And when wounded healed thy wound
   Sought thee wandering, set thee right
   Turned thy darkness into light

3. Can a woman's tender care
   Cease towards the child she bare
   Yes she may forgetful be
   Yet will I remember thee

4. Mine is an unchanging love
   Higher than the heights above
   Deeper than the depths beneath
   Free and faithful, strong as death

5. Thou shalt see my glory soon
   When the work of grace is done
   Partner of my throne shalt be
   Say poor sinner lov'st thou me

6. Lord it is my chief complaint
   That my love is weak and faint
   Yet I love Thee and adore
   O for grace to love Thee more

   Amen

HSS 48

1. Bless oh Lord the opening year
   To each soul assembled here
   Clothe Thy Word with power divine
   Make us willing to be Thine

2. Shepherd of Thy Blood-bought sheep
   Teach the stony hearts to weep
   Let the blind have eyes to see
   See themselves and look to Thee

3. Where Thou hast Thy work began
   Give new strength the race to win
   Scatter darkness, doubts and fears
   Wipe away the mourner's tear

4. Bless us all both old and young
   Call forth praise from every tongue
   Let this whole assembly prove
   All Thy power and all Thy love

   Amen

HSS 49

1. For thy mercy and Thy grace
   Faithful through another year
   Hear our song of thankfulness
   Father and Redeemer hear

2. Keep us faithful, keep us pure
   Keep us evermore Thine own
   Help, o help us to endure
   Fit us for the promised crown

3. So within the palace gate
   We shall praise on golden strings
   Thee, the only Potentate
   Lord of lords and King of kings

   Amen

HSS 50

1. Dear Lord and Father of mankind
   Forgive our foolish ways
   Re-clothe us in our rightful minds
   In purer lives Thy service find
   In deeper reverence praise

2. In simple trust like theirs who heard
   Beside the Syrian sea
   The gracious calling of the Lord
   Let us like them without a word
   Rise up and follow Thee

3. O Sabbath rest by Galilee
   O calm of hills above
   Where Jesus knelt to share with thee
   The silence of eternity
   Interpreted by love

4. Drop Thy still dew of quietness
   Till all our strivings cease
   Take from our souls, the stress and
   strain
   And let our ordered lives confess
   The beauty of Thy peace

5. Breathe through the heat of our desire
   Thy coolness and Thy balm
   Let sense be dumb, let flesh retire
   Speak through the earthquake, wind
   and fire
   O still small voice of calm!
   Amen

HSS 51

1. Great Shepherd of Thy people hear
   Thy presence now display
   As Thou hast given a place for prayer
   So give us hearts to pray

2. Within these walls let holy peace
   And love and concord dwell
   Here give the troubled conscience ease
   The wounded spirit heal

3. May we in faith receive Thy Word
   In faith present our prayers
   And in the presence of the Lord
   Unbosom all our cares

4. The hearing ear, the Seeing Eye
   The contrite heart bestow
   And shine upon is from on high
   That we in grace may grow

Amen

HSS 52

1. Be Thou my guardian and my guide
   And hear me when I call
   Let not my slippery footsteps slide
   And hold me lest I fall

2. The world, the flesh and satan dwell
   Around the path I tread
   O save me from the snares of hell
   Thou quickener of the dead

3. And if I tempted am to sin
   And outward things are strong
   Do Thou oh Lord, keep watch within
   And save my soul from wrong

4. Still let me ever watch and pray
   And feel that I am frail
   That if the tempter, cross my way
   Yet he may not prevail

Amen

HSS 53

1. Lead us heavenly Father, lead us
   O'er the world's tempestuous sea
   Guard us, guide us, keep us, feed us
   For we have no help but Thee
   Yet possessing every blessing
   If our God our Father be

2. Saviour breathe forgiveness o'er us
   All our weakness Thou dost know
   Thou dids't tread this earth before us
   Thou did'st feel its keenest woe
   Lone and dreary, faint and weary
   Through the desert, Thou didst go

3. Spirit of our God descending
   Fill our hearts with heavenly joy
   Love with every passion blending
   Pleasure that can never cloy
   Thus provided, pardoned, guided
   Nothing can our peace destroy

Amen

HSS 54

1. My God, my Father while I stray
   Far from my home, on life's rough way
   O teach me from my heart to say
   Thy will be done!

2. Though dark my path, and sad my lot
   Let me be still and murmur not
   Or breathe the prayer divinely taught
   Thy will be done!

3. If Thou shouldst call me to resign
   What most i prize, it ne'er was mine
   I only yield Thee what is Thine
   Thy will be done!

4. Let but my fainting heart be blest
   With Thy sweet Spirit for its guest
   My God to Thee I leave the rest
   Thy will be done!

5. Renew my will from day to day
   Blend it with Thine and take away
   All that now makes it hard to say
   Thy will be done!

6. Thy will be done
   Thy will be done
   O teach me from my heart t to say
   Thy will be done

Amen

HSS 55

1. Revive Thy work oh Lord
   Thy mighty arm make bare
   Speak with the voice that wakes the dead
   And make Thy people hear

2. Revive Thy work oh Lord
   Create soul-thirst for Thee
   And hungering for the Bread of life
   O may our Spirits be

3. Revive Thy work oh Lord
   Exalt Thy precious name
   And by Thy Holy Ghost our love
   For Thee and Thine inflame

4. Revive Thy work, O Lord
   Give Pentecostal showers
   The glory shall be all Thine own
   The blessing Lord be ours.

Amen

HSS 56

1. May the grace of Christ our Saviour
   And the Father's boundless love
   With the Holy Spirit's favour
   Rest upon us from above

2. Thus may we abide in union
   With each other and the Lord
   And possess in sweet communion
   Joys which earth cannot afford

Amen

HSS 57

1. Pass me not, O gentle Saviour,
   Hear my humble cry;
   While on others thou art calling,
   Do not pass me by.

   Savior, Saviour, hear my humble cry!
   While on others Thou art calling,
   Do not pass me by.

2. Let me at a throne of mercy
   Find a sweet relief;
   Kneeling there in deep contrition,
   Help my unbelief.

3. Trusting only in Thy merit,
   Would I seek Thy face;
   Heal my wounded, broken spirit,
   Save me by Thy grace.

4. Thou the spring of all my comfort,
   More than life to me,
   Whom have I on earth beside Thee?
   Whom in heaven but Thee?

Amen

HSS 58

1. There shall be showers of blessing
   This is the promise of love;
   There shall be seasons refreshing,
   Sent from the Saviour above.

   Showers of blessing, showers of blessing
   we need;
   Mercy drops round us are falling,
   But for the showers we plead.

2. There shall be showers of blessing
   Precious reviving again
   Over the hills and the valleys,
   Sound of abundance of rain.

3. There shall be showers of blessing
   Send them upon us oh Lord!
   Grant to us now a refreshing;
   Come and now honor Thy Word.

4. There shall be showers of blessing
   Oh that today they might fall,
   Now as to God we're confessing,
   Now as on Jesus we call!

Amen

HSS 59

1. Fill Thou my life oh Lord my God
   In every part with praise
   That my whole being may proclaim
   Thy being and Thy ways

2. Praise in the common things of life
   Its goings out and in
   Praise in each duty and each deed
   However small and mean

3. Fill every part of me with praise
   Let all my being speak
   Of Thee and of Thy love oh Lord
   Poor though I be and weak

4. So shalt Thou oh Lord receive from me
   The praise and glory due
   And so shall I begin on earth
   The song forever new

5. So shall each fear, each fret, each care
   Be turned into a song
   And every winding of the way
   The echo shall prolong

6. So shall no part of day or night
   Unblest or common be
   But all my life, in every step
   Be fellowship with Thee

Amen

CONSECRATION AND DEVOTION

HSS 60
1. Rock of Ages, cleft for me,
   Let me hide myself in Thee;
   Let the water and the blood,
   From Thy riven side which flowed
   Be of sin the double cure,
   Save me from its guilt and power.

2. Nothing in my hand I bring;
   Simply to Thy cross I cling!
   Naked, come to Thee for dress;
   Helpless look to Thee for grace;
   Foul, I to the fountain fly,
   Wash me savior or I die .

3. Not the labours of my hands
   Can fulfill Thy law's demands;
   Could my zeal no respite know,
   Could my tears forever flow,
   All for sin could not atone;
   Thou must save and Thou alone.

Amen

HSS 61
1. My hope is built on nothing less
   Than Jesus' blood and righteousness;
   I dare not trust the sweetest frame
   But wholly lean on Jesus' name.

   On Christ the solid Rock I stand;
   All other ground is sinking sand,
   All other ground is sinking sand.

2. When darkness hides His lovely face;
   I rest on His unchanging grace;
   In every high and stormy gale,
   My anchor holds within the veil.

3. His oath, His covenant, His blood,
   Support me in the 'whelming flood;
   When all around my soul gives way,
   He then is all my Hope and stay.

Amen

HSS 62
1. All to Jesus I surrender,
   All to Him I freely give;
   I will ever love and trust Him,
   In His presence daily live.

   I surrender all…. I surrender all;…
   All to Thee, my blessed Savior
   I surrender all…

2. All to Jesus I surrender,
   Humbly at His feet I bow;
   Worldly pleasures all forsaken
   Take me, Jesus, take me now.

3. All to Jesus I surrender,
   Make me Savior, wholly Thine;
   Let the Holy Spirit witness.
   I am Thine and Thou art mine.

4. All to Jesus I surrender;
   Now I feel the sacred flame;
   Oh the joy of full salvation!
   Glory, glory to His name.
   Amen

HSS 63
1. I am Thine, O Lord, I have heard Thy voice,
   And it told Thy love to me;
   But I long to rise in the arms of faith,
   And be closer drawn to Thee.

   Draw me near…er, nearer blessed Lord,
   To the cross where Thou hast died;
   Draw me nea…rer, nearer blessed Lor….d,
   To Thy precious, bleeding side.

2. Consecrate me now to Thy service Lord,
By Thy power of grace divine;
Let my soul look up with a steadfast hope,
And my will be lost in Thine.

3. There are depths of love that I cannot know
Till I cross the narrow sea,
There are heights of joy that I may not reach
Till I rest in peace with Thee.

Amen

HSS 64

1. Amazing grace! How sweet the sound
That saved a wretch like me;
I once was lost, but now I'm found;
Was blind but now I see.

2. T'was grace that taught my heart to fear
And grace my fears relieved;
How precious did that grace appear
The hour I first believed!

3. Through many dangers, toils and snares,
I have already come;
'Tis grace that brought me safe thus far,
And grace will lead me home.

4. Yes, when this heart ad flesh shall fail,
And mortal life shall cease,
I shall possess within the veil
A life of joy and peace

Amen

HSS 65

1. Take my life and let it be
Consecrated, Lord to Thee;
Take my moments and my days,
Let them flow in ceaseless praise.

2. Take my will and make it Thine
It shall be no longer mine:
Take my heart it is Thine own,
It shall be Thy royal throne.

3. Take my love, my Lord I pour
At Thy feet its treasure store:
Take myself and I will be
Ever, only, ALL for Thee.

Amen

HSS 66

1. When I survey the wondrous cross
On which the Prince of glory died
My richest gain I count but loss
And pour contempt on all my pride

2. Forbid it Lord, that I should boast
Save in the cross of Christ my God
All the vain things that charm me most
I sacrifice them to His Blood

3. See from His head, His hands, His feet
Sorrow and love flow mingling down
Did e'er such love and sorrow meet?
Or thorns compose so rich a crown

4. Were the whole realm of nature mine
That were an offering far too small
Love so amazing, so divine
Demands my soul, my life, my all

Amen

HSS 67

1. Lord I have made Thy Word my choice
My lasting heritage
There shall my noblest powers rejoice
My warmest thoughts engage

2. I'll read the histories of Thy love
And keep Thy laws in sight
While through the promises I rove
With ever fresh delight

3. 'Tis a broad land of wealth unknown
Where springs of life arise
Seeds of immortal bliss are sown
And hidden glory lies

4. The best relief that mourners have
It makes our sorrows blest
Our fairest hope beyond the grave
And our eternal rest
Amen

HSS 68

1. O for a closer walk with God
   A calm and heavenly frame
   A light to shine upon the road
   That leads me to the Lamb

2. Return, O Holy Dove, return
   Sweet messenger of rest
   I hate sins that made Thee mourn
   And drove Thee from my breast

3. The dearest idol I have known
   What e'er that idol be
   Help me to tear it from Thy throne
   And worship only Thee

4. So shall my walk be close to God
   Calm and serene my frame
   So purer light shall mark the road
   That leads me to the Lamb

   Amen

HSS 69

1. O Jesus I have promised
   To serve Thee to the end;
   Be thou forever near me,
   My Master and my Friend!
   I shall not fear the battle
   If Thou art by my side,
   Nor wander from Thy pathway
   If Thou wilt be my guide

2. O Jesus Thou hast promised
   To all who follow Thee,
   That where Thou art in glory
   There shall Thy servants be!
   And, Jesus, I have promised
   To serve Thee to the end;
   Oh, give me grace to follow
   My Master and my Friend

3. Oh let me see Thy foot marks,
   And in them plant mine own;
   My hope to follow duly
   Is in Thy strength alone.
   Oh, guide me, call me, draw me,
   Uphold me to the end;
   And then in heaven receive me,
   My Saviour and my Friend!

   Amen.

HSS 70

1. Christ is our Corner-stone,
   On Him alone we build;
   With His true saints alone
   The courts of heaven are filled:
   On His great love, our hopes we place
   Of present grace and joys above.

2. O then with hymns of praise
   These hallowed courts shall ring;
   Our voices we will raise
   The Three in One to sing;
   And thus proclaim, in joyful song,
   Both loud and long, that glorious
   name.

3. Here, gracious God do thou-
   For evermore draw nigh;
   Accept each faithful vow,
   And mark each suppliant sigh;
   In copious shower on all who pray
   Each holy day, Thy blessings pour.

   Amen

HSS 71

1. He that is down needs fear no fall
   He that is low no pride
   He that is humble ever shall
   Have God to be his guide

2. I am content with what I have
   Little be it or much
   And Lord, contentment still I crave
   Because Thou savest such

3. Fullness to such a burden is
   That go on pilgrimage
   Here little and hereafter bliss
   Is best from age to age

   Amen

HSS 72

1. Fight the good fight with all thy might
   Christ is thy strength and Christ thy
   right
   Lay hold on life and it shall be
   Thy joy and crown eternally

2. Running the race with God's good grace
   Lift up thine eyes and seek His face
   Life with its way before us lies
   Christ is the path and Christ the prize

3. Cast care aside, lean on Thy guide
   His boundless mercy will provide
   Trust and Thy trusting soul shalt prove
   Christ is it's life and Christ its love

4. Faint not nor fear, His arms is near
   He changeth not, and Thou art dear
   Only believe and thou shalt see
   That Christ is all in all to thee

   Amen

HSS 73

1. Christians seek not yet repose
   Hear thy guardian angel say
   Thou art in the midst of foes
        Watch and pray!

2. Gird thy heavenly armour on
   Wear it ever night and day
   Ambushed lurks the evil one
        Watch and pray!

3. Hear the victors who o'ercame
   Still they mark each warriors sway
   All in one sweet voice exclaim
        Watch and pray!

4. Watch above all, hear thy Lord
   Him thou lovest to obey
   Hide within thy heart His Word
        Watch and pray!

5. Watch as if on that alone
   Hung the issue of the day
   Pray that help may be sent down
        Watch and pray!

   Amen

HSS 74

1. Thine forever God of love
   Hear us from Thy throne above
   Thine forever may we be
   Here and in eternity

2. Thine forever, Lord of life
   Shield us through our earthly strife
   Thou the Life, the Truth, the Way
   Guide us to the realms of day

3. Thine forever, O how blest
   They who find in Thee their rest
   Saviour, Guardian, Heavenly Friend
   O defend us to the end

4. Thine forever, Thou our Guide
   All our wants by Thee supplied
   All our sins by Thee forgiven
   Lead us Lord, from earth to heaven

   Amen

HSS 75

1. Take up thy cross Thy Saviour said
   If thou would my disciple be
   Deny thyself, the world forsake
   And humbly follow after me

2. Take up thy cross in then His strength
   And calmly every danger brave
   'Twill guide thee to a better home
   And lead to victory o'er the grave

3. Take up Thy cross and follow Christ
   Nor think till death to lay it down
   For only He who bears the cross
   May hope to wear the glorious crown

4. To Thee, great Lord, the One in Three
   All praise forever more ascend
   O grant us in our home to see
   The heavenly life that knows no end

   Amen

HSS 76

1. Forth in Thy name o Lord I go
   My daily labour to pursue
   Thee only Thee, resolved to know
   In all I think or speak or do

2. The task Thy wisdom hath assigned
   O let me cheerfully fulfill
   In all my works Thy presence find
   And prove Thy good and perfect will

3. Give me to bear Thy easy yoke
   And every moment watch and pray
   And still to things eternal look
   And hasten to Thy glorious day

4. For Thee delightfully employ
   Whate'er Thy bounteous grace hath given
   And run my course with even joy
   And closely walk with Thee to heaven

   Amen

HSS 77

1. Breathe on me, Breath of God
   Fill me with life anew
   That I may love what Thou dost love
   And do what Thou wouldst do

2. Breathe on me, Breath of God
   Until my heart is pure
   Until with thee I will one will
   To do and to endure

3. Breathe on me, Breath of God
   Till I am wholly Thine
   Until this earthly part of me
   Glows with Thy fire divine

4. Breathe on me, Breath of God
   So shall I never die
   But live with Thee the perfect life
   Of Thine eternity

   Amen

HSS 78

1. When we walk with the Lord
   In the light of His Word,
   What a glory He sheds on our way!
   While we do His good will,
   He abides with us still,
   And with all who will trust and obey

   Trust and obey, for there's no other way
   To be happy in Jesus but to trust and
   obey

2. Not a shadow can rise
   Not a cloud in the skies,
   But His smile quickly drives it away;
   Not a doubt nor a fear,
   Not a sigh nor a tear,
   Can abide while we trust and obey.

3. But we never can prove,
   The delights of His love,
   Until all on the altar we lay;
   For the favour He shows,
   And the joy He bestows,
   Are for them who will trust and obey.

   Amen

HSS 79

1. Just as I am, without one plea,
   But that Thy blood was shed for me,
   And that Thou bidst me come to Thee,
   O Lamb of God I come, I come.

2. Just as I am, though tossed about
   With many a conflict, many a doubt,
   Fightings and fears within, without.
   O Lamb of...

3. Just as I am, thou wilt receive,
   Wilt welcome, pardon, cleanse, relieve;
   Because Thy promise I believe,
   O Lamb of...

4. Just as I am, Thy love unknown
   Has broken every barrier down,
   Now to be Thine, yea, Thine alone,
   O Lamb of God I come, I come.

   Amen

HSS 80

1. I need thee every hour,
   Most gracious Lord;
   No tender voice like Thine
   Can peace afford.

   I need Thee, oh I need Thee;
   Every hour I need Thee;
   Oh, bless me now, my Saviour!
   I come to Thee

2. I need Thee every hour
Teach me Thy will;
And Thy rich promises
In me fulfill.

3. I need Thee every hour,
Most Holy One;
Oh make me Thine indeed,
Thou blessed Son.

Amen

HSS 81

1. When upon life's billows you are
tempest tossed
When you are discouraged, thinking all
is lost,
Count your many blessings name them
one by one,
And it will surprise you what the Lord
hath done.

*Count...your blessings name them one
by one
Count ...your blessings see what God
hath done
Count... your blessings, name them one
by one
And it will surprise you what the Lord
hath done.*

2. Are you ever burdened with a load of
care
Does the cross seem heavy you are
called to bear?
Count your many blessings every doubt
will fly,
And you will keep singing as the days
go by.

3. So amid the conflict whether great or
small
Do not be disheartened God is over all;
Count your many blessings, angels will
attend
Help and comfort give you toy our
journey's end.

Amen

HSS 82

1. When all Thy mercies, O my God,
My rising soul surveys,
Transported with the view, I'm lost
In wonder, love and praise

2. Ten thousand thousand precious gifts
My daily thanks employ;
Nor is the least a cheerful heart.
That tastes those gifts with joy.

3. Through all eternity to Thee
A joyful song I'll raise;
But oh, eternity's too short
To utter all Thy praise.

Amen

HSS 83

1. Onward Christian soldiers! Marching as
to war,
Looking unto Jesus, who is gone before,
Christ the Royal Master, leads against
the foe,
Forward into battle, see His banners go.

*Onward Christian soldiers! Marching as
to war,
Looking unto Jesus, who is gone before.*

2. Like a mighty army, moves the church
of God
Brothers we are treading, where the
saints have trod;
We are not divided, all one body we,
One in hope and doctrine, one in
charity.

3. Onward then ye people, join our happy
throng
Blend with ours your voices, in the
triumph song;
Glory praise and honor, unto Christ the
King,
This though countless ages, men and
angels sing.

Amen

HSS 84

1. STAND up! Stand up for Jesus!
   Ye soldiers of the cross;
   Lift high His royal banner,
   It must not suffer loss;
   From victory unto victory
   His army He shall lead
   Till every foe is vanquished
   And Christ is Lord indeed

2. STAND up! Stand up for Jesus!
   The trumpet call obey;
   Forth to the mighty conflict
   In this His glorious day!
   Ye that are men now serve Him,
   Against unnumbered foes;
   Let courage rise with danger,
   And strength to strength oppose.

3. STAND up! Stand up for Jesus!
   Stand in His strength alone;
   The arm of flesh will fail you-
   Ye dare not trust your own
   Put on the gospel armour,
   And watching unto prayer'
   When duty calls or danger,
   Be never wanting there.

   Amen

HSS 85

1. Blessed assurance, Jesus is mine!
   Oh, what a foretaste of glory divine-
   Heir of salvation, purchase of God;
   Born of His Spirit, washed in His blood.

   This is my story, this is my song,
   Praising my Saviour all the day long;
   This is my story, this is my song,
   Praising my Saviour, all the day long.

2. Perfect submission, perfect delight,
   Visions of rapture now burst on my sight,
   Angels descending, bring from above,
   Echoes of mercy, whispers of love.

3. Perfect submission, all is at rest,
   I in my Saviour, I'm happy and blest,
   Watching and waiting, looking above,
   Filled with His goodness, lost in His love.
   Amen

HSS 86

1. STANDING on the promises of Christ my King.
   Through eternal ages let His praises ring
   Glory in the highest I will shout and sing
   Standing on the promises of God

   Stand...ing, Stand...ing,
   Standing on the promises of God my Saviour
   Stand...ing, Stan...ding...
   I am standing o the promises of God

2. Standing on the promises that cannot fail.
   When the howling storms of doubt and fear assail
   By the living Word of God I shall prevail,
   Standing on the promises of God

3. Standing on the promises of Christ the Lord,
   Bound to Him eternally by love's strong cord,
   Overcoming daily with the Spirit's sword,
   Standing on the promises of God.
   Amen

HSS 87

1. Put thou thy trust in God
   In duty's path go on
   Walk in His strength with faith and hope
   So shall thy work be done

2. Commit thy ways to Him
   Thy works into His hands
   And rest on His unchanging Word
   Who heaven and earth commands

3. Though years and years roll on
   His covenant shall endure
   Though clouds and darkness hide His path
   The promised grace is sure

4. Give to the winds thy fears
   Hope and be undismayed
   God hears thy sighs and counts thy tears
   God shall lift up thy head

5. Through waves and clouds and storms
   His power will clear the way
   Wait thou His time; the darkest night
   Shall end in brightest day

6. Leave to His Sovereign sway
   To choose and to command
   As shalt thou, wondering, own His way
   How wise, how strong His hand
   Amen

HSS 88

1. Nearer my God to Thee,
   Nearer to Thee
   E'en though it be a cross,
   That raiseth me
   Still all my song shall be
   Nearer my God to Thee
   Nearer my God to Thee
   Nearer to Thee

2. There let the way appear
   Steps unto heaven
   All that Thou sendest me
   In mercy given
   Angels to beckon me
   Nearer my God to Thee
   Nearer my etc.

3. Then with my waking thoughts
   Bright with Thy praise
   Out of my stony griefs
   Bethel I'll raise
   So by my woes to be
   Nearer, my God to Thee
   Nearer my etc.

   Amen

HSS 89

1. Thy kingdom come oh God
   Thy rule O Christ begin
   Break with Thine iron rod
   The tyrannies of sin

2. We pray Thee Lord arise
   And come in Thy great might
   Revive our longing eyes
   Which languish for Thy sight

3. Men scorn Thy sacred name
   And wolves devour Thy fold
   By many deeds of shame
   We learn that love grows cold

4. O'er heathen kinds afar
   Thick darkness broodeth yet
   Arise, O Morning Star
   Arise, and never set!

   Amen

HSS 90

1. When peace like a river attendeth my
   way
   When sorrows like sea billows roll
   Whatever my lot, Thou hast taught me
   to know
   It is well; it is well with my soul

   It is well.....with my soul
   It is well; it is well, with my soul

2. Though satan should buffet, though
   trials should come
   Let this blest assurance control
   That Christ hath regarded my helpless
   estate
   And hath shed His own blood, for my
   soul

3. My sin- oh the bliss of this glorious
   thought
   My sin- not in part, but the whole
   Is nailed to the cross; and I bear it no
   more
   Praise the Lord! Praise the Lord! Oh my
   soul

4. For me, be it Christ, be it Christ hence
   to live
   If Jordan above me shall roll
   No pangs shall be mine, for in death as
   in life
   Thou wilt whisper Thy peace to my soul

   Amen

HSS 91

1. Father I stretch my hands to Thee
   No other help I know
   If Thou withdraw Thyself from me
   Ah, wither shall I go?

   I do believe, I do believe
   That Jesus died for me
   And through His blood
   His precious blood
   I shall from sin be free

2. O Jesus, could I this believe
   I now should feel Thy power
   And all my wants Thou relieve
   In this accepted hour

3. Author of faith, to Thee I lift
   My weary, longing eyes
   Oh, let me now receive that gift
   My soul without it dies

   Amen

HSS 92

1. I could not do without Thee
   O Saviour of the lost,
   Whose precious blood redeemed me
   At such tremendous cost
   Thy righteousness, Thy pardon
   Thy precious blood must be
   My only hope and comfort
   My glory and my plea

2. I could not do without Thee
   I cannot stand alone
   I have no strength or goodness
   No wisdom of my own
   But Thou, beloved Saviour
   Art all in all to me
   And weakness will be power
   If leaning hard on Thee

3. I could not do without Thee
   For years are fleeting fast
   And soon in solemn loneness
   The river must be passed
   But Thou wilt never leave me
   And though the waves roll high
   I know Thou wilt be near me
   And whisper, it is I

   Amen

HSS 93

1. Seek ye first the kingdom of God
   And its righteousness
   And all these things shall be added unto you
   Allelu, Alleluia

2. Man shall not live by bread alone
   But by every Word
   That proceeds from the mouth of God
   Allelu, Alleluia

3. Ask and it shall be given unto you
   Seek and ye shall find
   Knock and the door shall be opened unto you
   Allelu, Alleluia

4. Seek ye first the kingdom of God
   And His righteousness
   And all these things shall be added unto you
   Allelu, Alleluia

   Amen.

HSS 94

1. Your only Son, no sin to hide
   But You have sent Him from Your side
   To walk upon this guilty sun
   And to become the Lamb of God

   O Lamb of God, sweet Lamb of God
   I love the Holy Lamb of God
   O wash me in, His precious blood
   My Jesus Christ,
   The Lamb of God

2. Your gift of love, they crucified
   They laughed and scorned Him as He died
   The humble King, they named a fraud
   And sacrificed the Lamb of God

3. I was so lost, I should have died
   But You have brought me to Your side
   To be led by, Your staff and rod
   And change my name, to the Lamb of God

HSS 95

Lord make us instruments of Your peace
Where there is hatred, let Your love
increase
Lord make us instruments of Your peace
Walls of pride and prejudice shall cease
When we are Your instruments of peace

1. Where there is hatred, we will show
His love
Where there is injury, we will never
judge
Where there is striving, we will speak
His peace
To the people crying for release
We will be His instruments of peace

2. Where there is blindness, we will pray
for sight
Where there is darkness, we will shine
His light
Where there is sadness, we will share
His grief
To the millions crying for release
We will be His instruments of peace

Amen

HSS 96

1. I know that my Redeemer lives
And ever prays for me
A token of His love He gives
A pledge of liberty

2. I find Him lifting up my head
He brings salvation near
His presence makes me free indeed
And He will soon appear

3. He wills that I should holy be
What can withstand His will?
The counsel of His grace
He surely shall fulfill

4. Jesus, I hang upon Thy Words
I steadfastly believe
Thou wilt return and claim me Lord
And to Thyself receive

Amen

HSS 97

1. All I once had dear, built my life upon
All this world with its, and was to own
All I once thought gain, I have counted
loss
Spent in worthless now, compared to
You

Knowing You, Jesus, knowing You
There is no greater thing
You're my all, You're the best
You're my joy, my righteousness
And I love You Lord

2. Now my heart's desire, is to know You
more
To be found in You, and all that's Yours
To possess Thy faith, what I could not
own
Also passing gifts of righteousness

3. Oh to know the power of Your risen life
And to know You in Your suffering
To become Thy true and Your daily
Word
So we live to live and never die

Amen

HSS 98

1. Jesus we Thy promise claim
We are gathered in Thy name
In the midst do Thou appear
Manifest Thy presence here

2. Sanctify us Lord and bless
Breathe Thy Spirit, give Thy peace
Come and dwell within each heart
Light and love and joy impart

3. Make us all in Thee complete
Make us all for glory meet
Fit to appear before Thy sight
Partners with the saints in light

Amen.

HSS 99

1. Praise the Saviour, ye who know Him
Who can tell how much we owe Him?
Gladly let us render to Him
All we are and have

2. Jesus, is the name that charms us
He is faithful, changing never
Nothing moves and nothing harms us
When we trust in Him

3. Trust in Him ye saints forever
He for conflicts fits ad arms us
Neither force nor guile can sever
Those He loves from Him

4. Keep us Lord, oh keep us cleaving
To Thyself and still believing
Till the hour of our receiving
Promised joys in heaven

5. Then we shall be where we would be
Then we shall be what we should be
Things which are not now, nor could be
Then shall be our own

Amen

3. And then one day
I'll cross the river
I'll find life's final world with pain
And this His death, gives way to victory
I'll see the light of glory and
I'll know He lives

Amen.

HSS 100

1. God sent His son
They called Him Jesus
He came to love, heal and forgive
He lived and died to buy my pardon
An empty grave is there to prove
My Saviour lives

Because He lives
I can face tomorrow
Because He lives
All fear is gone
Because I know
He holds my future
And life is worth a living
Just because He lives

2. How sweet to whom
The new born baby
And feel the crown, And joy He gives
But greater still, the calm assurance
This child can face on certain days
Because He lives

JUST WORSHIP

We are a worshipping Family. This is fully reflected in our name - Citizens Family Worship Ministries. Worship is the outpouring of deep affection and love to God. It is the complete abandonment of ourselves in the presence of our Heavenly Father.

Intimacy and oneness with God is the ultimate possibility of our redemption and relationship with Him. Any moment spent fully with God is the most blessed of all.

These songs are excellent for personal, as well as for corporate worship. Let our hearts and minds be raptured to a place of undistracted communion with God, through His blessed Holy Spirit, as we sing this songs alone, or in the company of our brethren.

Get this Classic Spiritual Resource from
Rev. Wildfire D-Favour

Can God Be Lonely?

A Life-transforming Encounter with the Holy Spirit

WD Favour

Can God Be Lonely?
A Life-Transforming Encounter with the Holy Spirit

Ever since 1994 when Wildfire D-Favour began to share his encounter with the Holy Spirit on a rainy night in the University of Nigeria, Nsukka, thousands of people have experienced tremendous personal revival in their walk with God.

This booklet contains that life-transforming revelation.

"I am more convinced today than ever before that intimate personal communion with God is the one single key that unlocks divine breakthroughs and supernatural favours."
~ Rev. Wildfire D-Favour

Available at all Citizens Family Church Offices

Just Worship Index

ADORATION, PRAISE, AND GRATITUDE

JW 1 | Here I am to worship

Light of the world You
stepped down into darkness
Open my eyes, let me see
Beauty that made this heart
adore You
Hope of a life spent with You

Chorus
Here I am to worship, here I am to bow down
Here I am to say that You're my God
Altogether lovely, altogether worthy
Altogether wonderful to me

King of all days, You're so
highly exalted
Glorious in heaven above
Humbly You came to the
earth You created
All for Your sake we can
know

I'll never know, how much
it cost
To see my sins upon that
cross

JW 2 | We have come into this place

We have come into this
place, gathered in Your
name to worship You
We have come into this
place gathered in Your name
to worship You
We have come into this
place gathered in Your name
to worship Christ the Lord
Worship Him, Jesus Christ
the Lord

Let's forget about ourselves,
concentrate on Him and
worship Him
Let's forget about ourselves,
concentrate on Him and
worship Him
Let's forget about ourselves,
concentrate on Him and
worship Christ the Lord
Worship Him, Jesus Christ
the Lord

JW 3 | Because of who You are

Because of who You are I
give You glory
Because of who You are I
give You praise
Because of who You are, I
will lift my voice and say
Lord I worship you because
of who You are

Refrain
Jehovah Jireh, my provider
Jehovah Nissi, Lord You reign
in victory
Jehovah Shalom, my Prince
of peace
And I worship You because
of who You are

JW 4 | No other name

No other name like the
name of Jesus
No other name like the
name of the Lord
No other name like the
name of Jesus
He's worthy of glory
He's worthy of honour
He's worthy of power and
praise

JW 5 | Lord I praise You

Lord I praise You because of
who You are
Not just for all the mighty
things that You have done
Lord I worship You because
of who You are
You are the reason why I
need to voice my praise
Because of who You are

JW 6 | I stand in awe of You

You are beautiful beyond
description,
Too marvelous for words
Too wonderful for compre-
hension
Like nothing ever seen or
heard
Who can grasp, Your infinite
wisdom
Who can fathom, the depth
of Your love
You are beautiful beyond
description
Majesty enthroned above

Chorus
I stand, I stand in awe of You
I stand, I stand in awe of You
Holy God to whom all praise is due
I stand in awe of You

JW 7 | You are fairer than the lilies

You are fairer than the lilies
of the valley
You are brighter than the
morning star
You are purer than the snow,
fresher than the breeze
You are lovelier by far than
all of these

JW 8 | I exalt You

For Thou oh Lord, art high
above all the earth
Thou art exalted far above
all the earth *2

Chorus
*I exalt You, I exalt You
I exalt you, Oh God *2*

JW 9 |Awesome God

Holy, are You Lord, all creation call you Lord
Worthy is Your name, we
worship Your majesty *2
Chorus

*Awesome God, how great
Thou art
You are Lord, mighty are
Your miracles
We stand in awe, of Your
holy name
Lord we bow and worship
You*

JW 10 | I exalt Your Holy name

I just want to praise You
I lift my voice to say, I love
You
You are everything to me
and I exalt Your holy name
I exalt Your holy name
I exalt Your holy name on
high

JW 11 | We sing praises to Your name

We sing praises to Your
name; oh Lord
Praises to Your name, oh
Lord
For Your name is great and
greatly to be praised
Praises to Your name, oh
Lord

Praises to Your name, oh
Lord
For Your name is great and
greatly to be praised

JW 12 | There is None like You

*There is none like You
No one else can touch my
heart like You do
I could search through all
eternity Lord and find
There is none like You*

Refrain
Your mercy flows like river
wide
And healing comes from
Your hand
Suffering children are safe in
Your arms
There is none like You

JW 13 | Forever You will be

All heavens declare the glory
of the risen King
Who can compare to the
beauty of the risen King
Chorus
*Forever You will be
The Lamb upon the throne
I'll gladly bow my knees
To worship You oh Lord*

JW 14 | Blessed be the Lord God Almighty

Father in heaven how we
love You
We lift Your name in all the
earth
May Your kingdom be established in our praises

As Your people, we declare
Your mighty works

Chorus
*Blessed be the Lord God
Almighty
Who was and is and is to
come
Blessed be the Lord God
Almighty
Who reigns forevermore*

JW 15 | Hallelujah

Hallelujah *3
For the Lord God Almighty
reigns
Hallelujah *3
For the Lord God Almighty
reigns
Hallelujah!

Chorus
*Holy! Holy! Are You Lord God
Almighty
Worthy is the Lamb, worthy
is the Lamb*2
Amen*

JW 16 | Your Majesty

I worship You,
In the beauty of holiness
I lift my voice to You,
For You are my righteous-
ness

Chorus
*You are royalty, so I crown
You King of Kings
Your Majesty, Your majesty*

I reverence You,
For only Thou art holy
I bow to You,
I'll forever sing Thy glory

JW 17 | How wonderful is Your name oh Lord

Chorus
*How wonderful is Your name oh Lord *2*
*How wonderful is Your name *2*
How wonderful is Your name oh Lord

Your name is sweeter than the morning dew
Your name is stronger than the raging storm
Your name is always there When I need a friend who cares
How wonderful is Your name oh Lord

Your name was given that I might go free
Your name has given me liberty
When all else seemed to be lost
I whispered Your sweet name
How wonderful is Your name oh Lord

JW 18 | Your Steadfast Love

Your steadfast love, extends to the heavens
Your faithfulness, reaches to the clouds
Your righteousness is like majestic mountains
And your wisdom like the depth of the seas
And you come to me

Filling my heart, with Your loving kindness
I find my peace, in the shadow of Your wings
I eat my fill from the abundance of Your household
And I drink from the streams of rejoicing
You are my King

JW 19 | Sometimes Hallelujah

Sometimes hallelujah
Sometimes praise the Lord
Sometimes gently sing
Our hearts in one accord

JW 20 | He is high and exalted

He is high and exalted
And worthy of praise
With our hearts we will love and adore
He is high and exalted
And worthy of praise
Holy is the Lord

Chorus
Holy! Holy! Holy is the Lord
Holy! Holy! Holy is the Lord

JW 21 | Majesty, Worship His Majesty

Majesty, worship His Majesty
Unto Jesus, be all glory, honor and praise
Majesty, kingdom authority
Flow from His throne, unto His own
His anthem raise

Refrain
So exalt, lift up on high the name of Jesus
Magnify, come glorify Christ Jesus the King

Majesty, worship His majesty
Jesus who died, now glorified *2
King of all kings

JW 22 | We Bless You Lord

We bless You Lord
We bless You Lord
We exalt You Lord
And magnify Your name

JW 23 | For the Lord is Holy

For the Lord is Holy
For the Lord is worthy
For the Lord is mighty
Lover of my soul *2

JW 24 | Above all powers

Above all powers, above all kings
Above all nature and all created things
Above all wisdom and all the ways of man
You were here before the world began

Chorus
Crucified, laid behind the stone
You lived to die, rejected and alone
Like a rose, trampled on the ground
You took the fall, and thought of me
Above all

Above all kingdoms, above all thrones
Above all wonders the world has ever known
Above all wealth and treasures of the earth
There's now way to measure what You're worth

JW 25 | It is good to praise the Lord

It is good to praise the Lord
It is good to gaze upon His majesty
To proclaim His love in the morning
And His faithfulness at night
Oh it is good to worship and praise*2
Oh it is good, to praise the Lord

JW 26 | Who is there like You, Oh God

Who is there like You, oh God
You created us in Your likeness
Who is there like You, oh God
You created us to be Your very own

Chorus
We lift our hands to the great I am
Who was and is and is to come
We lift our hands to the great I am
Who can compare with You

JW 27 | For You alone deserve all glory

You are the peace that floods my heart,
My help in times of need
You are the hope that leads me on
And brings me to my knees
For there I find You waiting
and there I find release
For with all my heart I worship
And unto You I sing

Chorus
For You alone deserve all glory
For You alone deserve all praise
Father we worship and adore You
Father we long to seek Your face
For You alone deserve all glory
For You alone deserve all praise
Father we love You, and we worship You this day

JW 28 | Joy of my desire

Joy of my desire
All-consuming fire
Lord of glory, Rose of Sharon
Reverence we
You are my Lord, my peace
Comforter and friend
Wonderful, so beautiful
You are to me

Chorus
I worship You
In Spirit and in truth *2
There will never be a friend

As dear to me as You

JW 29 | Glorify Your name

Father we love You, we worship and adore You
Glorify Your name in all the earth
Glorify Your name
Glorify Your name
Glorify Your name
In all the earth

JW 30 | We bring unto you our gratitude

We bring unto You
Our gratitude
We lift up our hearts in praise
We offer our lives
A sacrifice
As tokens our hands we raise

Chorus
Unto You
We minister unto You
You gave us beautiful garments of praise
So we minister unto You

JW 31 | Give thanks

Give thanks, with a grateful heart
Give thanks to the Holy One
Give thanks,
Because He's given,
Jesus Christ, the son *2

Chorus
And now, let the weak say I am strong,
Let the poor say I am rich

*Because of what the Lord has done for us *2*

Give thanks
We give thanks *2

JW 32 | Be glorified

Be glorified, be glorified
Be glorified, be glorified
Be glorified in the heavens
Be glorified in the earth
Be glorified in this temple
oh Lord
Jesus, Jesus, be thou glorified

JW 33 | Jesus we enthrone You

Jesus, we enthrone You
We proclaim You as King
Standing here in the midst
of all
We lift You higher with our
praise

Chorus
And as we worship, fill Your throne
And as we worship, fill Your throne
And as we worship, fill Your throne
Come Lord Jesus and take Your place

JW 34 | Bless the Lord oh my soul

Bless the Lord, oh my soul
And all that is within me,
bless His Holy name *2

He has done great things *3
Bless His Holy name

JW 35 | Shout to the Lord

My Jesus, my Saviour, Lord
there is none like You
All of my days, I want to
praise,
The wonders of Your mighty
hands
My Comfort, my Shelter
Tower of refuge and
strength
Let every breath, all that I
am
Never cease to worship you

Chorus
Shout to the Lord all the earth let us sing
Power and majesty, praise to the King
Mountains bow down and the seas will roar
At the sound of Your name
I sing for joy at the works of Your hands
Forever I'll love You, forever I'll stand
Nothing compare to the promise I have in You

JW 36 | We give You glory

We're here to bless Your
name, gathered as Your
family
To praise You and proclaim,
Your faithfulness and mercy

Chorus
We give You glory, we give
You honor
We give You everything we
are,
Lifting our hearts and hands
before You *2 (now)

We're here to seek Your
face, gathered in Your presence
To celebrate Your grace, to
praise Your for Your mercies

Refrain
There is no other reason
why we came
Than to glorify Your name
For You are worthy to be
praised
Now we offer up our life, as
a living sacrifice
Holy acceptable to You

JW 37 | In Humble Adoration

In humble adoration, we
bow before Your throne
As we come before Your
presence, we honor You
alone
So we lift up our voices, as
trumpets herald in You,
You are the King of Glory, so
this is what we do*2

Chorus:
*We worship You today*4*
*We honor You today*4*
*We love You today*4*
*We seek Your face today*4*

JW 38 | Your Majesty

I worship You,
In the beauty of holiness
I lift my voice to You,
For You are my righteousness

Chorus:
You are royalty
So I crown You King of kings
*Your Majesty *2*

I revere You,
For only Thou art holy
I bow to You,
I'll forever feel Your glory

JW 39 | You deserve the lifting of our hands

As we lift our hands to You,
It's an offering to You
And in liberty we worship
and we praise *2

Chorus
You deserve
You deserve
You deserve
*The lifting of our hands *2*

JW 40 | Here we are

Chorus
Here we are, lifting our
hands to You
Here we are, giving thanks
for all You do
As we praise and worship
Your holy name
You are here, dwelling within
our praise

For every answered prayer.
For always being there
For love that hears us when
we call
For arms that lift us when
we fall
You have always been, right
beside us
Leading us all along the way
We've made it through,
because of You

For days we cannot see
For all that's yet to be
The trials we may have to
face

When we'll be leaning on
Your grace
It will be Your strength that
saves us
Your love that makes us
strong
And through it all, we'll sing
this song

JW 41 | You are God and we praise You

You are God, and we praise
You
You are God, we adore You
You are the Lord Eternal
All creation worship You *3
Amen

JW 42 | Take this praise

All I am, You made me
All I have, You gave me
Take this praise, I offer unto
You
Everything, within me
And all I hope to be
Take this praise, I offer unto
You

JW 43 | But for Your grace

But for Your grace, I could
not be saved
But for Your grace, I'd go
my way
I'm forever grateful,
That You have been faithful
to me Lord
For Your amazing grace

JW 44 | I take this time

I take this time, to remem-
ber all of our love
I take this time, to say I'm
grateful Lord
I take this time, to count all
Your blessings in my life

Chorus
Halle Hallelujah
Halle Hallelujah
Halle Hallelujah
I'm grateful Lord.

JW 45 | All the glory must be to the Lord

While walking on this earth
We are nothing in ourselves
But the Master has chosen
to use us in His mighty hand
But the Master's plan may
require human instrument
But they must not ever
glorify themselves

Chorus
All the glory must be to the
Lord
For He is worthy of our
praise
No man on earth, should
give glory to himself
All the glory must be to the
Lord

JW 46 | Great is Your mercy

Great is Your mercy towards
me
Your loving kindness to-
wards me
Your tender mercies I see
Day after day

Forever faithful towards me
Always providing for me
Great is Your mercy towards
me
Great is Your grace

JW 47 | Jesus, how I love calling Your name

Jesus! Jesus! How I love,
calling Your name
Jesus! Jesus! Everyday, Your
name is the same

How I love, calling Your
name
Everyday, Your name is the
same

JW 48 | I will sing Holy

I will lift my voice and I will
sing
I will sing; Holy, holy
To my Lord and Saviour, my
God and King
I will sing; Holy, holy

Chorus
*I will praise the Lamb of God
who sits upon the throne
I will worship Him and sing
the praise to Him alone
He who was and is and is to
come
I will sing before His throne
Forever. Forever*

All the angels sing ad they
bow down
And they cry; Holy, holy
We Your sons and daugh-
ters, we praise You now
And we cry; Holy, holy

JW 49 | As a Father feeds His children

As a father feeds his children
Like a shepherd leads his
flock
The Lord will always guide
us
Show us where to walk
In times when we have
plenty
In times when we have
much
He is our provider
And His mercy never fails

Chorus
*Like a shepherd He leads us
Like a father, He feeds us
From the morning, till the
evening
Till the sunrise again
Like a shepherd He leads us
Like a father He feeds us
He is the great I am
He is the great I am*

JW 50 | Holy! Holy! Holy! Are You Lord

Can you hear the sound of
heaven
Like the sound of many
waters
It's the sound of worship,
coming from the throne
There are cries of adoration
As men from every nation
Lift their voice to make His
glory known
Singing

Chorus
*Holy! Holy! Holy! Are You
Lord
Holy! Holy! Holy! Are You
Lord*

Heaven and angels bow
Redeemed worship You now
*Holy! Holy! Holy! Are You
Lord*

JW 51 | Be magnified

I have made You too small in
my eyes
Oh lord, forgive me
And I have believed in a lie
That You are unable to help
me
But now oh Lord I see my
wrong
Heal my heart and show
yourself strong
And with my heart and in
my song
Oh Lord be magnified
Oh Lord be magnified

Chorus
*Be magnified oh Lord
You are highly exalted
And there is nothing You
can't do
Oh Lord my eyes are on You
Be magnified
Oh Lord, be magnified *2*

I have leaned on the wisdom
of men
Oh Lord, forgive me
And I have responded to
them
Instead of your love and
your mercy
But now oh Lord I see my
wrong
Heal my heart and show
yourself strong
And with my heart and in
my song
Oh Lord be magnified
Oh Lord be magnified

JW 52 | Because of Who You are

Lord I praise You because of
who You are
Not just for all the mighty
things that You have done
Lord I worship You because
of who You are
You are the reason why I
need to voice my praise
Because of who You

JW 53 | You are the peace I know

You are the peace I know
I don't want to worship from
afar
Shelter me in Your love
Your love is purer than my
heart

Chorus
How great You are
*How awesome You are *2*

Refrain
There is no higher mountain
No valley too deep
There is no river so wide
To keep me away from Your
love

There is a secret place
Where I can finally take my
place
In Your amazing grace
Holy Father, You are so great

JW 54 | Glory. Glory. To the Lamb

Glory
Glory
Glory to the Lamb *2

Chorus

For You are glorious and
greatly to be praised
You are the Lamb upon the
throne
And unto You I lift my voice
to sing
You are the Lamb upon the
throne

JW 55 | I worship You

I worship You
Almighty God, there is none
like You
I worship You
O Prince of peace
That is all I want to do
I give You praise
For You are my righteous-
ness
I worship You
Almighty God
There is none like You

JW 56 | There is None Like You

There is none like You
No one else can touch my
heart like You do
I could search through all
eternity Lord
And find, there I none like
You

Your mercies flow like a river
wide
Healing comes from Your
hand
Suffering children are safe in
Your arms
There is none like You

JW 57 | How excellent Your name is

O Lord and my God
How excellent Your name is
How excellent Your name in
*all the earth *2*

When I look into the heav-
ens
The moon and all the stars
I wonder what You ever saw
in me
That You took me and You
loved me
You've given me Your care
And I'll praise You
Through all eternity

JW 58 | Hosanna in the highest

Hosanna, in the highest
Let the King be lifted up
Hosanna

Be lifted higher, higher
Be lifted higher

Jesus You be lifted higher,
higher
Be lifted higher

JW 59 | You are Alpha and omega

You are Alpha and Omega
We worship you our God
You are worthy to be praised
*2

We give You all the glory
We worship You our God
You are worthy to be praised

JW 60 | Lord you reign forever

Lord You reign forever
You reign forever
I worship You
I worship You *2

You reign (echo) *8

JW 61 | No one like You

I stand amazed in Your presence
There is nothing You cannot do
I stand amazed in Your presence
There is joy, peace and all

Chorus
There's no one like You, Jesus
There's no one like You, in all the earth
There's no one like You, Jesus
There's no one like You

You do mighty things
You do glorious things
You're so faithful
Awesome is Your name *2

JW 62 | You are God

King of kings
Lord of lords
You are God *2

JW 63 | You reign in majesty

You reign in majesty
And Your name will ever be
The name above all names
Final authority

Chorus
For thine's the kingdom
And thine, the power
And thine, the glory
*Forever and ever *2*

JW 64 | We remember

We remember all You've done for us
We remember the blood You shed for us
We remember and worship You oh Lord

We remember the lonely nights You spent
We remember the lonely road You went
We remember and worship You oh Lord

We remember Your sacrifice for us
We remember the tears you shed for us
We remember and worship You oh Lord.

JW 65 | Lord I long to worship You

Lord I long to worship You
Lord I long to worship You
You have given me so much
To be thankful for
And my word is not enough
To express my love
Everything I have inside of me
Lord I give to You

There is nothing more to do
There is nothing more to do
There is nothing more to do
But worship You

JW 66 | I see the Lord

I see the Lord
I see the Lord
Exalted high above in worship
On the people of the earth
I see the Lord
I see the Lord
For mine eyes have see the King
The Lamb upon the throne
Who reigns forever

JW 67 | Hallowed be Your name

Holy Holy, Lord You're worthy
And I'm honored to sing Your praise
King of glory, Lord Almighty
Hallowed be Your name

All creation, every nation
Has it's being by Your Word
As it is done up in heaven
Let it be done here on earth
Let it be done here on earth

*Hallowed be Your name *3*
Lord and Majesty
Divine authority
Hallowed be Your name

JW 68 | Oh Lord I receive Your love

Oh Lord, Your tenderness
Melting all my bitterness
Oh Lord, I receive Your love
Oh Lord, Your loveliness
Hiding all my ugliness
Oh Lord I receive Your love

Oh Lord I receive Your love
Oh Lord, I receive Your love

PASSION FOR HIS PRESENCE

JW 69 | I'm desperate for You

This is the air I breathe *2
Your holy presence, living in me
This is my daily bread *2
Your very Word, spoke to me

Chorus:
And I……., I'm desperate for You
And ……….I, I'm lost without You

JW 70 | All glory, all honour, all power

All Glory. All Honour. All Power
To You
All Glory. All Honour. All Power
To You
Holy Father, we worship You
Blessed Jesus, my Saviour
Holy Spirit, we wait on You
Holy Spirit we wait on You
For fire *2

JW 71 | Fill my heart Lord

Fill my heart Lord
I lift it up Lord
Come and quench
This thirsting of my soul
Bread of heaven
Fill me till I want no more
Fill my heart, Fill it up
And make me whole

JW 72 | I will keep my mind stayed on You

I will keep my mind stayed on You
I will keep my eyes fixed on You
You will keep my heart in perfect peace
When I think of You *2

JW 73 | Because You are everything to me

Because You are, everything to me
Because You are, everything to me
So I lift Your name on high
So I lift Your name on high

JW 74 | Lord You are more precious than silver

Lord You are more precious than silver
Lord You are, more costly than gold
Lord You are, more beautiful than diamond
There is nothing I desire compared to You

JW 75 | You're the sole desire of my heart

You're the sole desire of my heart *2
Still more with every passing day
As things of earth just pass away
I've come to know the joy of loving You
You're the sole desire of my heart

You're the sole desire of my heart *2

Lord speak to me I'm standing still
I've come to You reveal Your will
I'll listen to Your voice and then obey
You're the sole desire of my heart

JW 76 | We bow down and confess

We bow down and confess,
You are God in this place
We bow down and confess,
You are God in this place

Chorus
You are all I need. It's Your face I seek
I the presence of the King
We bow down, we bow down

JW 77 | Down at Your feet Oh Lord

Down at Your feet oh Lord,
Is the most high place
In Your presence Lord
I seek Your face, I seek Your face

Chorus
There is no higher calling,
No greater honor
Than to bow and kneel before Your throne
I'm amazed at Your glory,
Embraced by Your mercy
Oh Lord, I live to worship You

JW 78 | Jesus Lamb of God

You are my strength when I
am weak
You are the treasure that I
seek
You are my all in all
Seeking You as a precious
jewel
Lord to give up I'd be a fool
You are my all in all

Chorus
*Jesus, Lamb of God, worthy
is Your name
Jesus, Lamb of God, worthy
is Your name*

Taking my sin, my cross, my
shame
Rising again I'll bless Your
name
You are my all in all
When I fall down You picked
me up
When I am dry You fill my
cup
You are my all in all

JW 79 | You are awesome in this place

As I come into Your
presence,
Pass the gates of praise
Into Your sanctuary,
We are standing face to face
I look upon Your
countenance, I see the
fullness of Your grace
I can only bow down and say

Chorus
*You are awesome in this
place, mighty God
You are awesome in this
place, Abba Father
You are worthy of our praise,
to You our hearts we raise
You are awesome on this
place, mighty God*

JW 80 | Jesus, You're the centre of my joy

Jesus, You're the centre of
my joy
All that's good and perfect
come from You
You're the heart of my desire, hope of all I do
Jesus, You're the centre of
my joy

JW 81 | I'm coming back to the heart of worship

When the music fades and
all is stripped away
And I simply come
Longing just to bring, an of-
fering that's of worth
That'll bless Your heart

Refrain
*I'll bring You more than a
song,
For a song in itself, is not
what You have desired
You search much deeper
within,
Through the way things
appear
You're looking into my heart*

Chorus
*I'm coming back to the heart
of worship
It's all about You, It's all
about You Jesus
I'm sorry Lord for the thing
I've made it,
It's all about You, it's all
about You Jesus*
King of endless words, no
one could express
How much You deserve

Though I'm weak and bored,
all I have is Yours
Every single breath

JW 82 | All I want is more of You

All I want is more of You
All I want is more of You
Nothing I desire dear Lord
But more of You

Jesus I am thirsty
Won't You come and fill me
Earthly things have made
me dry
Only You can satisfy
My heart is crying out
For more of You
For more of You

JW 83 | Reign in me

Captivate my heart o Lord
Let Your will be done in my
life
Establish here Your throne
Let Your kingdom come

Chorus
*Reign in me
Sovereign Lord
Reign in me*

JW 84 | Lord I thirst for you

Lord I thirst for You
And I long to be in Your
presence
My soul will wait on You
Father draw me nearer,
draw me nearer
To the beauty of Your holi-
ness

Chorus

I will wait on You, Almighty God
In the beauty of Your holiness
I will worship You, Almighty God
In the beauty of Your holiness

JW 85 | Oh Lord I long to know Your glory

Lord my heart is the temple of Your spirit
Let my spirit feel the warmth of Your embrace
Lord I am, Your holy habitation
Where Your Spirit is pleased to dwell

Chorus
Oh Lord I long to know, Your glory
I want to offer, the sacrifice of praise
Fill this temple Lord
With Your Spirit, once again

JW 86 | More love, more Power

More love, more power
More of You in my life *2
Chorus
I will worship You with all of my heart
I will worship You with all of my mind
I will worship You with all of my strength
You are my God

JW 87 | Draw me close to You

Draw me close to You, never let me go
I lay it all down again, to hear You say that I'm Your friend
You are my desire, no one else will do
Nothing else can take Your place
To feel the warmth of Your embrace
Help me find a way, bring me back to You

Chorus
You're all I want
You're all I ever needed
You're all I want
Help me know You are near

JW 88 | Let the rain of Your presence fall on me

Let the rain of Your presence fall on me
Everyday that I live, with every breath I breathe
Let the rain of Your presence, fall on me
Everywhere that I go
Lord let Your presence flow
Rain on me

Chorus
Love divine, joy unspeakable
Overflow, within my soul
This heart of mine, is refreshed and at rest
In Your presence
In Your presence

JW 89 | Lord Your glory fills this atmosphere

Lord Your glory fills this atmosphere
Lord Your glory fills this atmosphere
As we worship and as we praise
It fills this atmosphere
As we worship and as we praise
It fills this atmosphere

JW 90 | Lord You are welcome in this place

Lord You are welcome in this place
Lord You are welcome in this place
Lord You are welcome in this place
Have Your way

Move by Your Spirit *3
Send Your anointing *3
Heal and deliver *3

JW 91 | Here I am waiting

Here I am waiting, abide in me I pray
Here I am longing for You
Hide me in Your love
Bring me to my knees
May I know Jesus, more and more

Chorus
Come live in me, all my life
Take over
Come breathe in me and I will rise
On eagle's wings

JW 92 | We thirst for You

We thirst for You, we search for You
In a dry and barren land,
We're longing for Your hand
To guide us to,
A place where You
Can cleanse us with Your rain,
Baptize us once again
We thirst for You

Oh Lord we are waiting, let Your river flow
Comfort our hearts again
Quench our thirsty souls

JW 93 | To keep Your lovely face

To keep Your lovely face,
ever before my eyes
This is my prayer today
Lord make it my sole desire
That in my secret place
No other love competes, no rival throne survives
And I'll serve only You

JW 94 | Open the eyes of my heart Lord

Open the eyes of my heart Lord
Open the eyes of my heart Lord
I want to see You
I want to see You *2

Chorus
To see You high and lifted up
Shinning in the light of Your glory
Pour out Your power and love
*As we sing Holy, Holy, Holy *2*

*Holy! Holy! Holy! *3*
I want to see You

JW 95 | Come Holy Spirit we need You

Come Holy Spirit we need You
Come sweet Spirit we pray
Come in Your strength and Your power
Come in Your own special way

JW 96 | Zion is calling you to a higher place of praise

Zion is calling you, to a higher place of praise
To stand upon this mountain top
And magnify His name
To tell all His people, every nation that He reigns
Zion is calling you, to a higher place of praise

Chorus
It becomes the highest praise
When all that I am, responds to who You are
It becomes the highest praise
Just to know You Lord

JW 97 | I love You more than anything

I love You
More than anything
I love You
More than life itself
I love You
Lord I give my life to You

JW 98 | I pour my love on You

I don't know how, to say exactly how I feel
I can't begin to tell You what Your love has made
I'm lost for words
Is there a way to show the passion in my heart
Can I express, how truly great I think You are
My dearest friend
Lord this is my desire, to pour my love on You

Chorus
Like oil upon Your feet
Like wine for Your to drink
Like water from my heart
I pour my love on You
If praise is like perfume
I'll lavish mine on You
Till every drop is gone
I pour my love on You

JW 99 | You are the love of my life

You are, the love of my life
You are, the hope that I cling to
You mean more than this world to me
I wouldn't trade You, for silver or gold
I wouldn't trade You, for riches untold
You are, You are my everything

I couldn't take one step
without You
I could never go on
I couldn't live one day with-
out You
'Cos I don't have the
strength
To make it on my own

JW 100 | Jesus Lover of my soul

Jesus, lover of my soul
Jesus, I will never let You go
You've taken me, out of the
miry clay
Set my feet upon the rock
and now I know
I love You, I need You
Though my world may fall,
I'll never let You go
My Saviour, my closest
friend
I will worship You until the
very end

JW 101 | O the glory of His presence

O the glory of His presence
We Your temple, Give You
reverence
Come and rise from Your rest
And be blended by our
praise
As we glory, In Your embrace
As Your presence now fills
this place
Jesus, all glorious
Create in us a temple
Carved on living stones
Where you're enthroned
As you rose from death in
part
So rise within our worship
Rise upon our praise

And let the hands that you
saw raised
Clothe us in your glory
Guide us by your grace

JW 102 | You are the fire in me

You are the fire in me
You are the power at work
in me
You are my ever present
helper
Holy Spirit I adore

Chorus
Precious Holy Ghost
I worship You, I worship You
Precious Holy Ghost
Come take your place in me

JW 103 | Jesus, Your presence makes me whole

Jesus, oh Jesus *3
Your presence makes me
whole

JW 104 | We are standing on holy ground

We are standing, on holy
ground
And I know that there are
angels, all around
Let us praise, Jesus Christ
We are standing in God's
presence on holy ground

JW 105 | I enter the Holy of holies

I enter the holy of holies

I enter through the blood of
the Lamb
I enter to worship you only
I enter to honour I am

Chorus
Lord I worship you
*I worship You *2*
For Your name is holy
*Holy, Holy Lord. *2*

JW 106 | In Your presence, that's where I belong

Chorus
In Your presence, that's
where I belong
In Your presence, oh Lord
my God
In Your presence, that's
where I am strong
Seeking Your face, touching
Your grace
In the cleft of the rock
In Your presence oh Lord

I want to go where the rivers
cannot overflow me
Where my feet are on the
rock
I want to hide where the
blazing fire cannot burn me
In Your presence oh God

I want to hide where all the
flood of evil cannot reach
me
Where I am covered by the
blood
I want to be where the
schemes of darkness cannot
touch me
In Your presence O God

JW 107 | Father we declare that we love you

And we will say, that You are good
And all the miracles You've done have brought us joy
And we are changed
And all the hopes we have we place in You right now

Chorus
Father we declare, that we love You
We declare our everlasting love for You

We lift up our eyes above the troubles in our lives
And together we stand to declare You as King
In times like this, we choose to praise You
For it's You, it's You who really matter
You are worthy of our praise

JW 108 | Have Your way

Have Your way
Have Your way
Holy Spirit fill our hearts
And have Your way
As we pray
And as we wait
Speak Your word into our hearts
And have Your way

JW 109 | You are my song

You are my song. You are song

You are the reason I sing
You are the reason I sing
You are my song, You re my song
You are the reason, I sing today

JW 110 | In Your presence, I am content

In Your presence, I am content
In Your presence, I am content
In Your presence, there is life
Expressions of Your love
Revelations of Your power and might
In Your presence, I may bring
A love song offering
I'm in the presence of my King

JW 111 | Open the floodgates of heaven

Let it rain
Let it rain
Open the floodgates of heaven
Let it rain
Let it rain

JW 112 | I'm here to say, I love you

I've come to say how much I love You
I've come to say how much I adore You
Lord I'm not here to complain, about my many problems
By Your Spirit and Your grace I'm confident You'll solve them

Chorus
I'm here to say, I love You
I'm here to say I adore You
I'm here to say, I love You
I long to love You Lord

I've come to say how much I need You
The longing of my heart is to please You
Let Your all consuming fire, cleanse me in Your presence
Lord my heart and my desire, is to serve and give You reverence

JW 113 | Spirit of the Sovereign Lord

Spirit of the Sovereign Lord
Come and make Your presence known
And reveal the glory the Living God *2

Chorus
Let the weight of Your glory cover us
Let the life of Your river flow
Let the truth of Your kingdom reign in us
Let the weight of Your glory
Let the weight of Your glory fall

JW 114 | You make my life so beautiful

You make my life so beautiful
And as You are, You have made me here on earth
There's nothing greater than this
That's why I love You, forever more *2

Chorus
*I want more of You *2*
Jesus
The more I know You
The more I want to know
You, Jesus
More of You

JW 115 | You make me lie down in green pastures

You make me lie down
In green pastures
You make me wanting
For nothing
You fill my hunger
With honey from Your sweet
sweet Word
You make me worship,
before You
So I will love and adore You
You are my Shepherd
You are my Jesus
You are my Lord

JW 116 | All I want is more of You

All I want is more of You
All I want is more of You
Nothing I desire dear Lord
But more of You
Jesus I am thirsty
Won't You come and fill me

Chorus
Earthly things have left me dry
Only You can satisfy
My heart is crying out
For more of You
For more of You

JW 117 | When I look into You holiness

When I look into Your holiness
When I gaze into Your loveliness
When all things that surround me
Become shadows in the light of You
When I find the joy of reaching Your heart
When my will becomes enthralled in Your own
When all things that surround me
Become shadows in the light of You

Chorus
I worship You
I worship You
*The reason I live, is to worship You *2*

JW 118 | We worship You in the spirit

We worship You in the spirit
We worship in the truth
We worship You in the spirit
That's what we're gonna do *2

Into the holy of holies
That's where I want to be

JW 119 | I love you Lord

I love you Lord
And I lift my voice
To worship You, oh my soul rejoice
Take joy my king
In what you hear

Let it be a sweet, sweet sound in your ear.

JW 120 | You are the reason I live

You are the reason I live
You are the One for me
You are the One for me

Why should I fear when I've got You
Surrounded by Your love
Your everlasting love
Why should I care what people say
They don't know, what You mean to me

You are the One for me *4

JW 121 | Deeper in love

There is a longing, only You can fill
A raging tempest, only You can still
My soul is thirsty Lord, to know You as I'm known
Drink from the river, that flows before Your throne

Chorus
Take me deeper
Deeper in love with You
Jesus hold me close in your embrace
Take me deeper
Deeper than I've ever been before
I just want to love you more and more
How I long to be deeper in love

Sunrise to sunrise, I will seek Your face
Drawn by the Spirit, to the promise of Your grace
My heart has found in You, a hope that will abide
Here in Your presence, forever satisfied

JW 122 | More of You

More of You
And less of me
Lord I pray that there might be
More of You, and less of me

JW 123 | You are lovely

Master, Maker, life Creator come
And dwell in me
That my life may know Your tender mercies
Shine through me that all may see Your love
So full and free
And I'll declare Your praise
Through endless ages

Chorus
You are lovely
You are Holy
Gave supremely
That all men might see
You are gentle
Tender-hearted
Risen Savior
You are God

JW 124 | Our Hearts, Our Desire

Heavenly Father, Your mercy showers
Down upon all people

Every ray upon the earth
May Your Spirit pierce the darkness
Break the chains of death upon us
Let us rise in earnest worship
To declare Your matchless worth

Chorus
Our hearts, our desire
Is to see the nations worship
Our hearts, our desire
Is to sing Your praise to the ends of the earth
That with one mighty voice
Every tribe, every tongue rejoicing
Our hearts, our prayer
Is to see the nations worship You

JW 125 | Come and take Your place oh Lord

Come and take Your place oh Lord
Deep within my heart
Take the place that's Yours oh Lord
Deep within my heart
And of the increase
Of Your government

*There shall be no end *3*
You are worthy Lord to be praised

JW 126 | As the deer

As the deer panteth for the waters
So my soul longs after You
You alone are my heart's desire

And I long to worship You

Chorus
You alone are my strength and shield
You alone will my Spirit please
You alone are my heart's desire
And I long to worship You

You're my friend and You are my brother
Even though You are my King
I love You more than anybody
And I love to worship You

JW 127 | In Moments like this

In moments like this
I sing out a song
Is sing out a love song to Jesus
In moments like this
I lift up my eyes
I lift up my eyes
To the Lord

Singing I love You Lord
Singing I love You Lord
Singing I love You Lord
I love You

JW 128 | Yesterday is gone

Yesterday is gone
Today is here
And we're standing in Your presence
Lifting holy hands in one accord
All I want to do is worship You

Worship You like never
before
Worship You oh Lord like
never before

Chorus
More than I did yesterday *2
All I want to do is worship
You like never before *2

JW 129 I will come and bow down

I will come, and bow down
At Your feet Lord Jesus
In Your presence is fullness
of joy
There is nothing
There is no one
To compare with You

I take pleasure in worshipping *3
You Lord

JW 130 | Holy is the Lamb

What will you do, when you
see Jesus?
What will you do, when you
see Jesus?

Chorus
I'll sing Holy! Holy!
I will join the host of angels
and sing holy!
I'll sing Holy! Holy!
Is the lamb upon the throne

I'll sing for joy, when I see
Jesus

I'll cry for joy when I see
Jesus

Refrain
Holy is the lamb, upon the
throne
Worthy is the lamb, upon
the throne

HEALING and MIRACLES

JW 131 | For You are great

You deserve the glory, and
the honor
Lord we lift our hands in
worship
As we praise Your holy name
...Repeat
Chorus
For You are great,
You do miracles so great
There is no one else like You
There is no one else like You
...Repeat

JW 132 | You are my hiding place

You are my hiding place, You
always fill my heart
With songs of deliverance,
whenever I am afraid
I will trust in You, I will trust
in You
I confess that I am strong
In the strength of the Lord

JW 133 | He will come and save you

Say to those who are fearful
hearted

Say to those who are broken
hearted
Do not be afraid
The Lord your God is strong
And prevails mightily
He will come and save

Chorus
He will come and save you
*2
Say to the weary one
Your God will surely come
He will come and save You
*2
Lift up your eyes to Him
You will arise again
He will come and save you

JW 134 | I know that I can make it

You don't have to worry
And don't you be afraid
Joy comes in the morning
Troubles they don't last
always

Refrain:
Remember there's a friend
in Jesus
Who will wipe your tears
away
And if your heart is broken
Just lift those hands and say

Chorus
Oh, I know that I can make it
I know that I can stand
No matter what
May come my way
My life is in Your hands

You have trials and troubles
They seem to weigh you
down
All your friends and lovers
Are nowhere to be found
(Refrain)

JW 135 | There's a river that flows

There's a river that flows
From the fountain of life
And it heals everything
along
The way
I have tested and known
That for every broken heart
There is healing in Jesus
name

JW 136 | There is a fountain

There is a fountain filled
with blood
Drawn from Emmanuel's
veins
Where sinners plunged
Beneath that flood
Loose all their guilty stains

Chorus
He is the Son
Of the living God
He's Jesus Christ
The Holy One
Where sinners plunged
Beneath that flood
Loose all their guilty stains

The dying thief rejoiced to
see
That fountain in His day
And there may I
Though vile as he
Wash all my sins away

Chorus
He is the Son
Of the living God
He's Jesus Christ

The Holy One
And there may I
Though vile as he
Wash all my sins away

When this poor lisping stam-
mering tongue
Lies silent in the grave
Then in a nobler sweeter
song
I'll sing Thy power to save

Chorus
He is the Son
Of the living God
He's Jesus Christ
The Holy One
Then in a nobler
Sweeter song
I'll sing Thy power to save

JW 137 | Jesus is the answer

Jesus is the answer, for the
world today
Above Him there's no other,
Jesus is the way *2

JW 138 | There can be miracles

Many nights we prayed
With no proof anyone could
hear
In our hearts a hopeful
We barely understood
Now we are not afraid
Although we know there's
much to fear
We were moving mountains
long
Before we knew we could

Chorus
There can be miracles

When You believe
Though hope is frail
It's hard to kill
Who knows what miracles
You can achieve
When you believe
Somehow you will
You will when you believe

In this time of fear
Hope seems like a summer
ball
That's slipping all the way
Now I'm standing here
Hearts so full, I can't explain
Seeking faith and speaking
words
I never thought I'd say

JW 139 | There is something about Your name

Jesus! Jesus! Jesus,
There is something about
Your name
Master! Saviour! Jesus!
Like the fragrance after the
rain
Jesus! Jesus! Jesus!
Let the heavens and earth
proclaim
Kings and kingdoms shall all
pass away
But there's something about
that name

JW 140 | In the presence of Jehovah

In the presence, of Jehovah
God Almighty, Prince of
peace
Troubles vanish, hearts are
mended
In the presence, of the King

Chorus
In Your presence, in Your holy presence
The weary and the burdened rest
The broken are restored
In Your presence, in Your holy presence
There's nothing like the presence of the Lord
Come boldly in to the presence of the Lord

JW 141 | Suddenly a touch from heaven

Like the woman with the issue of blood
We press in, we press in
Like the blind man, waiting patiently
We press in, through the crowd

Chorus
Suddenly! A touch from heaven
Jesus came and rescued me
Suddenly! A touch from heaven
Jesus came, and set me free

JW 142 | He is able, more than able

He is able, more than able
To accomplish what concerns me today
He is able, more than able
He can handle anything that comes my way
He is able, more than able

To do much more than I could ever dream
He is able, more than able
To make me what He wants me to be

JW 143 | Be it unto me according to your word

Be it unto me, according to Your Word
According to Your promises I can stand secured
Carve upon my heart, the truth that sets me free
According to Your Word oh Lord
Be it unto me

You promised Your Word will deliver
Lord we believe its true
You promised us joy like a river
Lord we receive it from You
The things You have spoken
They're coming to pass
This world's disappearing
But Your Word will last

JW 144 | God can do it again

God can do it again
And again and again
He's the same God today
As He's always has been
Yesterday and today
And forever the same
There's no reason to doubt
God can do it again

JW 145 | As we worship in Your presence, there is healing

As we worship in Your presence, there is healing
The Holy Spirit's gentle touch, is flowing
Jesus, we believe
Jesus, there is healing in Your name

Refrain
Almighty Father, we lift our hands to You
To receive Your power
To do as You would do

JW 146 | You won't leave here like you came

You won't leave here, like you came
Bound, oppressed, tormented, sick or lame
For the Holy Ghost of old is still the same
You won't leave here like you came in Jesus name

JW 147 | He touched me

He touched me
He touched me
And oh, what joy that feels my soul
Something happened
And I know
He touched me and made me whole

JW 148 | The presence of the Lord is in this place

You will never leave same way you came

For the power of the Lord is here to change
You will never leave same way you came
For the power of the Lord is here to change
You will never be the same

The presence of the Lord is in this place (echo) *2
The power of the Lord is in this place (echo) *2
The glory of the Lord is in this place (echo) *2

I can feel His power over me
His anointing changing me *2
My life will never be the same *3
For the presence of the Lord is in this place.

JW 149 | I am the Lord that healeth thee

I am the Lord that healeth thee
I am the Lord your healer
I sent My Word, and healed your disease
I am the Lord, your healer
You are the Lord that healeth me
You are the Lord my healer……

JW 150 | What's that you have in your hands

When you have a work to do
And the task ahead seems bigger than you
That's when He steps in

When you know in your heart that God's command
Takes more than can be done by man
That's when He steps in
He sees you at the point of your need
He sees you at the point of crossing your Red sea
In the moment you call
When you've given your all
He steps in, He steps in

Chorus
And He'll say, what's that you have in your hand
I can use it, if you're willing to lose it
Take the little you have and make grand
I am Elshaddai
And I'll more than supply your need

When all you have is oil in a jar
That's a reflection of where you are
That's when He steps in
A little boy's lunch of fish and bread
Is all you have for the need ahead
That's when He steps in
Let Him, take it and bless it
And break it and give it
He'll multiply it, in the moment you give it
In the moments you call
When you've given all
He steps in, He steps in

JW 151 | You've Healed me oh Lord

You've healed me oh Lord
And now I am healed

You've saved me and now I am saved
You've healed me oh Lord
And now I am healed
You are the One I praise
You are the One I praise

JW 152 | His presence is here to heal

His presence is here
To heal
His presence is here
To heal
For I am the Lord
That healeth thee
His presence is here
To heal

Be healed
Be healed
In the presence of the Lord
Be healed *2

THE CROSS AND CONSECRATION

JW 153 | My body is Your sanctuary

My body is Your sanctuary, my body is Your sanctuary
Purify me like a gold so I might be bold to say
My body is Your sanctuary

JW 154 | Lord I give you my heart, I give you my soul

This is my desire, to honor You
Lord with all my heart I worship You

All I have I within me, I give You praise
All that I adore is in You

Chorus
Lord I give You my heart, I give You my soul
I live for You alone
Every breath that I take, every moment I'm awake
Lord have Your way in me

JW 155 | Lord prepare me, a sanctuary

Lord prepare me, a sanctuary
Pure and holy, tried and true
With thanksgiving, I'll be a living
Sanctuary, for You

JW 156 | I just set aside the cares of this world

I just set aside the cares of this world
To fall in love with You again
I just throw away the burdens of this world
To fall in love with You

Chorus
I'm in love with You *4

JW 157 | The pattern of this world

The pattern of this world
I will deny it
The pattern of this world
I will defy it
Lord renew my mind
That I can find
That good and perfect will

Lord I offer up my body
As a living sacrifice

Holy and pleasing to You *2

JW 158 | Come and make my heart Your home

Come and make my heart Your home
Come and be everything I have and all I own
Search me through and through
Till my heart becomes, Home for You

Chorus
A home for You
A home for You
Let everything I do, open up a door for Your to come through
Till my heart will be, a place where you want to be

JW 159 | Emmanuel

I was born to be, Your dwelling place
A home for the presence of my King
So let my life now be, separated unto You
That I might, what I was born to be

Chorus
Emmanuel, Emmanuel
Your name is called, Emmanuel
God with us, living in us
Your name is called, Emmanuel

JW 160 | Shepherd of my soul

Shepherd of my soul, I give You full control
Wherever You may lead I will follow
I have made a choice to listen to Your voice

Wherever You may lead I will go

Chorus
Be it in the quiet pasture or by the gentle streams
Shepherd of my soul is by my side
Should I face a mighty mountain or the valley dark and deep
Shepherd of my soul, will be my guide

JW 161 | In My Life, Lord be glorified

In my life Lord
Be glorified
Be glorified
In my life Lord
Be glorified
Today

JW 162 | I will make my life Your dwelling place

I will make my life Your dwelling place
I will build Your throne in my life
Come Father, Come Son
Come Holy Spirit
Come and take Your place in my life

JW 163 | Change my heart oh God

Change my heart oh God, make it ever true
Change my heart oh God, may I be like You

You are the Potter, I am the clay
Melt me and mould me
This is what I pray

JW 164 | Lord I offer my life to you

Chorus
Lord I offer my life to You
Everything I've been through
Use it for Your glory
Lord I offer my days to You
Lifting my praise to You
As a pleasing sacrifice
Lord I offer You my life

Things in the past. Things
yet unseen
Visions and dreams that are
yet to come true
All of my hopes and all of
my past
My heart and my hands, I lift
it to You.

All that I am, all that I have
I lay them down before You
oh Lord
All my request , and all of
my plans
I lay them down, I bring
them to You

JW 165 | By Your blood

By Your blood, You have
saved us
By Your blood, You re-
deemed us
By Your blood, we can enter
Into Your holy place
By Your blood, You have
saved us
By Your blood, You re-
deemed us
By Your blood,
Precious blood of the Lamb

JW 166 | Now let the Son of God enfold you

Oh, let the Son of God
enfold you

with his spirit and his love.
Let him fill your heart and
satisfy your soul.
Oh, let him have the things
that hold you
and his spirit, like a dove,
Will Descend upon your life
and make you whole.

Chorus
Jesus, oh Jesus,
Come and fill your lambs.
Jesus, oh Jesus
Come and fill your lambs.

Oh, come and sing this song
with gladness
As your hearts are filled with
joy.
Lift your hands in sweet sur-
render to his name
Oh, give him all your tears
and sadness
Give him all your years of
pain
And you'll enter into Life in
Jesus' name.

JW 167 | Hold me close, let your love surround me

Lord I've come to You, let my
heart be changed; renewed
Flowing from the grace, that
I've found in You
Lord I've come to know, the
weaknesses I see in me
Will be stripped away
By the power of Your love

Chorus
Hold me close, let Your love
surround me
Bring me near, draw me to
Your side
And as I wait, I'll rise up like
the eagle
And I will soar with You, Your
Spirit leads me on

By the power of Your love

Lord unveil my eyes, let me
see You face to face
The knowledge of Your love,
as You live in me
Lord renew my mind, as
Your will unfolds in my life
And living everyday, by the
power of Your love

JW 168 | Lord I'm available to You

Lord, I'm available to You
My will I give to You
I'll do what You say do
Use me Lord
To show someone the way
And enable me to say
My storage is empty
And Lord I'm available to
You

JW 169 | Though I walk through valleys low

I walk closer now on the
higher way
Through the darkest night
Would You hold my hand
Jesus, guide my way
Would you mourn with me
And you'd dance with me
For my heart of hearts
Is bound to You

Chorus
Though I walk through val-
leys low
I fear no evil
By the waters still my soul
My heart will trust in You

Oh You counsel me
And You comfort me
When I cannot see
You light my way

JW 170 | Holy Spirit rain down

Holy Spirit rain down, rain down
O Comforter and friend
How we need Your touch again
Holy Spirit rain down, rain down
Let Your power fall
Let Your voice be heard
Come and change our hearts
As we stand on Your Word
Holy Spirit rain down

No eye has seen
No ear has heard
No mind can know
What God has in store
So open up heaven
Open it wide
Over the church
And over our lives

JW 171 | Falling in love with Jesus

Falling in love with Jesus
Falling in love with Jesus
Falling in love with Jesus
Was the best thing I ever,
Ever done

In His arms, I feel protected
In His arms, never disconnected
In His arms, I feel protected
There's no place I'd rather
Rather be

JW 172 | Spirit touch Your church

Spirit touch Your church
Stir the hearts of men
Revive us Lord
With Your passion once again
I want to care for others
Like Jesus cares for me
Let Your rain fall upon me

Lord we need Your grace and mercy
We need to pray like never before
We need the power of the Holy Spirit
To open heaven's doors

JW 173 | In His time, He makes all things beautiful

In His time
In His time
He makes all things beautiful
In His time
Lord please show me everyday
As you're teaching me Your way
That we do just what You say
In Your time

JW 174 | I Surrender all to You

I've given You my heart
And all that is within
I lay it all down
For the sake of You my King
I've given You my dreams
I'm laying down my last
I'm giving up my price
For the promise of new life

Chorus
And I surrender, all to You
All to You *2

I'm singing You this song
I'm waiting at the cross
All the world holds dear
I count it all as loss
For the sake of knowing You
For the glory of Your name
The know the lasting joy
In sharing in Your pain

JW 175 | On the night He was betrayed

On the night He was betrayed He took the bread
After giving thanks He broke it and said

This is my body
Broken for you
And as you eat it
Remember me (2x)

On the night He was betrayed He took the cup
After lifting it He blessed it and said
This is my blood
Poured out for you
And as you drink it
Remember me (2x)

JW 176 | By Your blood

By Your blood You have saved us
By Your blood You've redeemed us
By Your blood we can enter
In to Your Holy Place
By Your blood You have saved us

By Your blood You've re-
deemed us
By Your blood
Precious blood of the Lamb.

JW 177 | Father we have confidence

Father we have confidence
By the blood of Jesus Christ
To come into the place
where you are
To come into the place
where you are.

By the New and Living way
We enter into the holy
place,
To Worship You with all our
hearts,
To worship You with all Our
hearts.

JW 178 | Jesus You are the sweetest name of all

Jesus You are the sweetest
name of all
Jesus You always hear me
when I call
Jesus You pick me up each
time I fall
You're the sweetest
The sweetest name of all.

Jesus, how I love to praise
Your name
Jesus, you're still the first,
the last, the same
Oh, Jesus, You died and took
away my shame
You're the sweetest, sweet-
est name of all

Jesus, You're the soon and
coming King

Jesus, we need the love that
You can bring
Oh, Jesus, we lift our voices
up and sing
You're the sweetest, sweet-
est name of all

JW 179 | Be exalted Oh Lord

Be exalted Oh Lord
Above the heavens
And let Your glory
Be over all the earth (2x)

Let Your glory
Let Your glory
Let Your glory
Be over all the earth (2x)

JW 180 | All that is within me Lord

All that is within me Lord
Will bless Your holy name
I live my life to worship You
alone
You brought me out of dark-
ness
Into Your glorious light
Forever I will sing of Your
great love *2

Chorus
Holy! Holy! Holy is the Lord
Holy! Holy! Holy is the Lord

I love to see You glorified
To see You lifted high
I yearn to see all nations
bow their knees
It's You alone Lord Jesus
who
Can cause the coldest heart
To find Your love and ever-
lasting peace *2

JW 181 | Bread of life, sent down from glory

Bread of life, sent down
from glory
Many things You were on
earth
A holy King, a carpenter
You are the living Word

Awesome Ruler, gentile
Redeemer
God with us a living truth
And what a friend we have
in You
You are the living Word

Jesus! Jesus! that's what we
call You
Manger born, hung on a
tree
You died to save humanity
You are the living Word

Oh oh oh……………….
You are the living Word *4

JW 182 | I can do all things

I can do all things
Through Christ who gives
me strength
But sometimes I wonder
what He can do through me
No great success to show
No glory of my own
Yet in my weakness, He's
there to let me know

Chorus
His strength is perfect when
all strength is gone
He carries us when we can't
carry on

Rest in His power, the weak
becomes strong
His strength is perfect *2

His strength in us begins
When ours come to an end
He hears our humble cry
and proves again

JW 183 | With my hands lifted up

With my hands lifted up
And my mouth filled with
praise
With a heart of thanksgiving
I will bless You oh Lord

Chorus
I will bless You oh Lord *2
With heart of thanksgiving
I will bless You oh Lord

JW 184 | Every time that we are gathered

Intro:
As we gather may Your Spirit
dwell within us
As we gather may we glorify
Your name
Knowing well that as our
hearts begin to worship
We'll be blessed because we
came
Oh Lord, we'll be blessed
because we came

Every time that we are
gathered
Together in His name
There He is awesome in
power and in strength
So let us continually offer
A sacrifice to Him
For it is good to give praises
to our King

Chorus
For He inhabits the praises
of His people
So let our praises be sweet
incense unto You
Let the lifting of our hands
Be as the evening sacrifice
Lord we love You
Oh yes, we love You *2
Yes we do

JW 185 | Here we are

Here we are in Your pres-
ence

Lifting holy hands to You
Here we are praising Jesus
For the things He's brought
us through

JW 186 | Jesus, just the mention of Your name

Jesus, just the mention of
Your name
Flowers grow and the desert
blooms again
Like fire in winter cold
Like pure precious gold
Jesus, just the mention of
Your name

JW 187 | Jesus, Jesus Lord to me

Jesus Jesus Lord to me
Master, Saviour, Prince of
peace
Ruler of my heart today
Jesus, Lord to me

JW 188 | It is Jesus

It is Jesus,
Yes it is Jesus
Yes it is Jesus in my soul

For I have touched
The hem of His garment
And His blood, has made me
whole

General Index

A

Above all powers   63
Alleluia, sing to Jesus!   39
All glory, all honour, all power   70
All hail the power of JESUS NAME!
   32
All I once had dear, built my life upon
   55
All I want is more of You   71, 76
All people that on earth do dwell   30
All that is within me Lord   85
All the glory must be to the Lord   66
All to Jesus I surrender,   46
Amazing grace! How sweet the sound
   47
As a father feeds His children   67
A safe stronghold our God is still   29
As the deer   77
As we worship in Your presence, there
   is healing   80
At the name of Jesus, every knee shall
   bow   36
Awesome God   62

B

Because of who You are   61
Because You are everything to me   70
Be exalted Oh Lord   85
Be glad in the Lord and rejoice,   33
Be glorified   65
Be it unto me according to your word
   80
Be magnified   67
Be Thou my guardian and my guide
   44
Blessed assurance, Jesus is mine!   52
Blessed be the Lord God Almighty   62
Bless oh Lord the opening year   43
Bless the Lord oh my soul   65

Bread of life, sent down from glory
   85
Breathe on me, Breath of God   50
But for Your grace   66
By Your blood   83, 85

C

Christians seek not yet repose   49
Christ is our Corner-stone,   48
Come and make my heart Your home
   82
Come and take Your place oh Lord   77
Come Holy Spirit we need You   73
Come Thou Almighty King   30

D

Dear Lord and Father of mankind   43
Deeper in love
   Take me deeper   76
Down at Your feet Oh Lord
   There is no higher calling   70
Draw me close to You
   You're all I want   72

E

Emmanuel   82
Every time that we are gathered   86

F

Falling in love with Jesus   84
Father I stretch my hands to Thee   54
Father of mercies on Thy Word   36
Father we declare that we love you
   And we will say that you are good
   75
Father we have confidence   85
Father we love you
   Glorify Your name   64
Fight the good fight with all thy might
   48
Fill my heart Lord   70
Fill Thou my life oh Lord my God   45

N

O

P

R

S

T

There is something about Your name
79
There's a river that flows   79
There shall be showers of blessing   45
Thine forever God of love   49
Though I walk through valleys low
83
Thou whose Almighty Word   29
Thy kingdom come oh God   53
To God be the glory! Great things He
hath done   31
To keep Your lovely face   73

W

We are standing on holy ground   74
We Bless You Lord   63
We bow down and confess   70
We bring unto you our gratitude
Unto You; we minister unto you   64
We give You glory   65
We have come into this place   61
We plough the fields and scatter   38
We remember   69
We sing praises to your name   62
We thirst for You   73
We worship You in the spirit   76
What a friend we have in Jesus   35
What's that you have in your hands
When you have a work to do   81
When all Thy mercies, O my God,   51
When I look into You holiness   76
When I survey the wondrous cross   47
When peace like a river attendeth my
way   53
When upon life's billows you are
tempest tossed   51
When we walk with the Lord   50
Who is He in yonder stall?   31
Who is there like You, Oh God   64
With my hands lifted up   86

Y

Ye servants of God, your Master pro-

claim   41
Yesterday is gone   78
You are Alpha and omega   68
You are awesome in this place   71
You are fairer than the lilies   61
You are God   69
You are God and we praise You   66
You are lovely   77
You are my hiding place   78
You are my song   75
You are the fire in me   74
You are the love of my life   73
You are the peace I know   68
You are the reason I live   76
You deserve the lifting of our hands
66
You make me lie down in green pas-
tures   76
You make my life so beautiful
I want more of you Jesus   76
You reign in majesty   69
You're the sole desire of my heart   70
Your Majesty   62, 65
Your only Son, no sin to hide   54
Your Steadfast Love   63
You've Healed me oh Lord   81
You won't leave here like you came
80

Z

Zion is calling you to a higher place of
praise   73

www.ingramcontent.com/pod-product-compliance
Lightning Source LLC
Chambersburg PA
CBHW030813150426
42813CB00069BA/3333/J